CANADIAN WILDS

LECTOR HOUSE PUBLIC DOMAIN WORKS

CANADIAN WILDS

MARTIN HUNTER

ISBN: 978-93-5420-523-1

Published: -

LECTOR HOUSE LLP
E-MAIL: lectorpublishing@gmail.com

CANADIAN WILDS

TELLS ABOUT
THE HUDSON'S BAY COMPANY,
NORTHERN INDIANS
AND
THEIR MODES OF HUNTING,
TRAPPING, ETC.

BY

MARTIN HUNTER

CONTENTS

Chapter		Page
	INTRODUCTION	ix
I.	THE HUDSON'S BAY COMPANY	1
II.	THE "FREE TRADER."	4
III.	OUTFITTING INDIANS	8
IV.	TRACKERS OF THE NORTH	11
V.	PROVISIONS FOR THE WILDERNESS	15
VI.	FORTS AND POSTS	18
VII.	ABOUT INDIANS	21
VIII.	WHOLESOME FOODS	24
IX.	OFFICERS' ALLOWANCES	28
X.	INLAND PACKS	31
XI.	INDIAN MODE OF HUNTING BEAVER	34
XII.	INDIAN MODE OF HUNTING LYNX AND MARTEN	39
XIII.	INDIAN MODES OF HUNTING FOXES	42
XIV.	INDIAN MODES OF HUNTING OTTER AND MUSQUASH	45
XV.	REMARKABLE SUCCESS	48
XVI.	THINGS TO AVOID	51
XVII.	ANTICOSTA AND ITS FURS	55
XVIII.	CHISELLING AND SHOOTING BEAVER	58
XIX.	THE INDIAN DEVIL	62

XX. A TAME SEAL. 66

XXI. THE CARE OF BLISTERED FEET. 70

XXII. DEER-SICKNESS.. 72

XXIII. A CASE OF NERVE. 76

XXIV. AMPHIBIOUS COMBATS. 79

XXV. ART OF PULLING HEARTS. 83

XXVI. DARK FURS. 86

XXVII. INDIANS ARE POOR SHOTS. 90

XXVIII. A BEAR IN THE WATER. 92

XXIX. VORACIOUS PIKE. 94

XXX. THE BRASS-EYED DUCK. 96

XXXI. GOOD WAGES TRAPPING. 99

XXXII. A PARD NECESSARY.. 102

XXXIII. AN HEROIC ADVENTURE. 104

XXXIV. WILD OXEN. 108

XXXV. LONG LAKE INDIANS. 110

XXXVI. DEN BEARS. 113

XXXVII. THE MISHAPS OF RALSON.. 116

MARTIN HUNTER

INTRODUCTION.

By the courtesy of Forest and Stream and Hunter-Trader-Trapper these articles are republished in book form by the author.

I have been induced to bring them out a second time under one cover by the frequent requests of my fellow bushmen who were kind enough to criticise them favorably when they first appeared in the magazine.

In this preamble I think it proper and possibly interesting to the reader to have a short synopsis of my career.

I entered the service of the Hudson's Bay Company in 1863 as a clerk and retired in 1903 a commissioned officer of twenty years' standing.

The modes of Trapping and Hunting were learned directly by personal participation in the chase with the Indians and the other stories heard first hand from the red man.

My service in the employ of the Great Fur Company extended from Labrador in the East to Fort William on Lake Superior in the West and from the valley of the St. Lawrence in the South to the headwaters of its feeders in the North.

By canoes and snowshoes I have traveled on the principal large rivers flowing south from the height of land, among them I may mention the Moisee, Bersimis, St. Maurice, Ottawa, Michipocoten, Pic and Nepigon.

I have hunted, trapped and traded with the Montagnais, Algonquins and Ojibways, the three largest tribes that inhabit the country mentioned in the foregoing boundaries and therefore the reader can place implicit reliance in what is herein set forth. Giving a synopsis of the history of The Hudson's Bay Company, its Forts and Posts and the Indians they traded with as well as other incidents of the Canadian wilds.

Respectfully,
MARTIN HUNTER.

CANADIAN WILDS.

CHAPTER I.

THE HUDSON'S BAY COMPANY.

The Hudson's Bay Company was incorporated in the year 1670 and received its charter from Charles the Second, making it today the longest united company that ever existed in the world.

In 1867 when the different provinces of old Canada were brought under the Dominion Confederation, the Company ceded its exclusive rights, as per its charter, to the government of Canada, making this vast territory over which the Company had held sway for nearly two hundred years, free for hunters, trappers and traders.

Prince Rupert, of England, was associated with the first body of "Adventurers Trading into Hudson's Bay," for such were they designated in the charter and the charter gave them the right to trade on all rivers and their tributaries flowing into Hudson's Bay.

They established their first forts or factories at the mouths of the principal rivers that fall into the bay on the east, south and west shores, such as East Main, Rupert's, Moose, Albany, Churchill and a few intermediate small outposts along the seashore. They endeavored to draw the interior Indians down to the coast to trade but after a few years they found that the long journey to the factories took up so much of the Indian's time and left them, after their return to their hunting grounds, so exhausted from their strenuous exertions in negotiating the turbulent and swift flowing waters, that the company's management decided to stretch out and establish trading places up the different rivers.

This small beginning of a post or two up each river was gradually continued ever further south, ever further west, as the requirements of the fur trade necessitated, there the company pushed in and followed their own flag, a blood red ground with H. B. C. in white block letters in the center.

This flag is known from Labrador to the Pacific and from the St. Lawrence river to the Arctic regions. Several would-be wits have given these mysterious letters odd meanings. Among several I call to memory, "Here Before Christ," "Hungry Belly Company" and "Here Before Columbus."

Two ships visited the Bay each summer bringing supplies for the next winter and taking back to England the furs and oil collected during the past season. The coming of these ships, one to York Factory and the other to Moose Factory, was the event of the year as they brought the only mail the "Winterers" received from friends and relatives in far away Old England.

Navigating the Bay was done pretty much by the rule of "Thumb." Notwithstanding its being one of the most dangerous bodies of water in America it is wonderful (now that the Bay is fairly well charted and shows up most of the dangerous reefs and shoals) how few accidents these old navigators had in taking their ships in and out of the Bay.

Much depended on those same ships reaching their destination. Starvation would confront the officers and servants in the country and the want of the returns in England during those early days of the venture would have been a serious setback to their credit. While the ships were in the roadstead unloading and loading it was an anxious time to the captain and the officer ashore for as the work had to be done by lighters (the ship lying three miles from the land) there was always the danger of a strong wind springing up. In such events the boats scurried ashore while the ship slipped her cable and put to sea till fair weather.

In parting with their charter to the Canadian Government the company reserved certain acreages about each and every one of their forts and posts besides two sections in each township from the Lake of the Woods to the Rocky Mountains and from the international boundary line to the northern edge of the Fertile Belt. These reserves of land sold to the incoming settlers as the country is filling up is a great source of revenue to the share holders and are becoming more and more valuable each succeeding year.

Where most of the old prairie posts stood in the old days, the company now have "Sale Shops" for the whites and at these places they are successfully meeting competition, by the superiority and cheapness of the goods they supply.

In old Canada the fur trade had always been the principal commerce of the country and after the French regime several Scotch merchants of Montreal prosecuted it with more vigor than heretofore. This they did under the name of "The Northwest Company." Their agents and "Couriers des Bois" were ever pushing westward and had posts strung from Ottawa to the Rocky Mountains and all the pelts from that immense country were brought yearly to the headquarters in Montreal.

The Hudson's Bay Company after having inhabited all the territory that they could rightly claim under their charter, began to oppose the Northwest Company in the country they had in a way discovered. The Hudson's Bay Company after getting out of the Bay found the Northwest Company's people trading on the Red, Assiniboine and Saskatchewan, all rivers that they could claim by right of their charter seeing they all drained into Hudson's Bay and then began one of the keenest and most bloody commercial warfares in history.

Might was right and wherever furs were found the strongest party, for the time being, took them. Retaliation was the unwritten law of the country and what was this week a Hudson's Bay post was next week occupied by a party of North-westers or vice versa. There is hardly a place in what is now the peaceful and law abiding Manitoba and the western provinces but what, if it could tell the tale, had witnessed at some time in its early history sanguinary conflicts between the two powerful and rival companies.

Things got to such a pass that the heads of the two fur parties in London and Montreal saw that something had to be done to stay this loss of lives and goods. Arrangements were therefore made that the majority of the stockholders of both companies should meet in London. This convention had its first meeting on the 19th of May, 1821, and several other assemblies of the two factions took place before all the points at issue were mutually agreed upon.

By wide mindedness and a liberal amount of give and take between the two contending parties a full understanding was agreed on. One of the points upon which a strong objection was made was the sinking of one of the identities, but this knotty point was eventually settled. A coalition of the two companies was formed under the title of "The Hudson's Bay Company," the first official year of the joined parties dating first of June, 1821, and the first governor, Mr. George Simpson, afterwards "Sir George."

Mr. Simpson was knighted by Queen Victoria for having traveled from Montreal to London by land with the exception of crossing Behring Strait and the English Channel by boat.

Sir George Simpson held the position of Governor of the fur trade of the Hudson's Bay Company for very many years and was followed by Governors Dallas, McTavish, Graham and Sir Donald A. Smith (now Lord Strathcona) after the latter's term of office the title of this position was altered to "The Commissioner." The first gentleman to hold the management under this new title was Mr. Wriggley, who after serving two terms of four years each, retired and was succeeded by Mr. C. C. Chipman who is still in office and brings us down to the present day.

There has always been a Governor and committee in London where the real headquarters has ever been, while the Commissioner's head place in Canada is situated in Winnipeg.

The whole of the Great Company's collection of furs is shipped to England and sold by auction three times a year, in January, March and October. Buyers from all over Europe attend these sales.

CHAPTER II.
THE "FREE TRADER."

The origin of the term "Free Trader" dates back considerably over three-quarters of a century and was first used as a distinction by the Hudson's Bay Company between their own traders, who traded directly from their posts and others who in most cases had been formerly in their employ, but had turned "Free Traders." Men with a small outfit, who roamed amongst the Indians on their hunting grounds and bartered necessary articles that the hunters were generally short of.

The outfit mostly consisted of tobacco, powder, ball, flints, possibly one or two nor' west guns, white, blue and red strands for the men's leggings, sky blue second cloth for the squaw's skirts, flannel of several bright colors, mole skin for trousers, a few H. B. cloth capots, fancy worsted sashes, beads, ribbons, knives, scissors, fire steels, etc. Some of the foregoing articles may not be considered necessary requirements, but to the Indian of those days they were so looked upon and a "Free Trader" coming to an Indian's camp who had the furs, a trade, much to the trader's profit was generally done.

In those away back days the Free Trader was always outfitted by the "Great Company." He endured all the labor, hardships and privation of following the Indians to their far off hunting grounds and of a necessity charged high for his goods. Being a former servant of the company he got his outfit at a reduced price from what the Indians were charged at the posts. The barter tariffs at each of the posts was made out in two columns, i. e., Indian Tariff and Free Man's Tariff. Say, for example, a pound of English tobacco was bartered to the Indian at the posts for one dollar a pound, the Free Trader would get it in his outfit for 75 cents, and when he bartered it to some hunter, probably hundreds of miles off, he would charge one and half to two dollars for the same pound of tobacco.

I mention, to illustrate the amount in dollars and cents, but the currency of those days all over the northwest and interior was the "Made Beaver." As a round amount the M. B. was equivalent to 50 cents of our money of today. At all the posts on Hudson's Bay the company had in coinage of their own, made of brass of four amounts; an eight, quarter, half and whole Beaver. The goods were charged for at so many or parts of Made Beaver and the furs likewise valued at the same currency.

Like most uneducated men who have to remember dates, people and places, these Free Traders had wonderful memories. One who had been away on his venture for eight or ten months could on opening his packs, tho there might be two or three hundred skins in his collection, if so requested, tell from what particular Indian he received any skin picked out at haphazard.

Observation and remembrance entered into every phase of their lives as it does into that of the pure Indian. Their very lives at times depended on their faculties and one might say all their bumps were bumps of locality and these highly developed all the way back from childhood.

Of their nationality they were mostly French Canadians or French half breeds, and as a rule went on their trading expeditions accompanied by their Indian wives and children. Time was of no object and as they traveled they trapped and hunted as they went. Their very living and subsistence depended on their guns and nets. Loaded as they were with goods to trade and their necessary belongings they could not take imported provisions. After their hardships of several months, after the breaking up of the lakes and rivers, they once more found themselves at the post from whence they received their outfit.

From the factor down to the old pensioners, the people of the fort went down to welcome the new arrivals. Their advent was heralded by the firing of guns on rounding the point at which they first came in view of the post. On landing a general handshaking was gone thru by the two parties, the factor mentally estimating the probable contents of the rich packs.

The men, engaged servants, of the post, carried up to the house the peltries, while the Free Traders followed the factor to the trade shops where a plug of tobacco for the men and sugar for the women were given out by the clerks and with a generous tot of rum in which to cement their continued friendship, the Free Trader took his departure to put up his tepee and get his family and belongings under cover.

Later on the servants brought him pork, lard, flour and tea enough for him and his family for supper and breakfast. No accounts were gone into on the day of arrival. The next morning, however, the Trader repaired to the store with the factor and his clerk, the latter carrying his ledger and day blotter. The pads being unlaced the different kinds of skins were placed in separate piles and then classified according to value. The sum total being arrived at the amount of his outfit and supplies being deducted he was given a "bon" on the trade shops for his credit balance.

Shortly after the Free Trader and his wife would be seen in the shop decking themselves out with finery, bright and gay colored clothes and fixings were the first consideration. After if there still remained a credit, luxuries in the eating way were indulged and that night a feast given by the Free Traders to the employes and hangers on at the post.

Yes, they were a jolly, childlike race of men and as improvident as an Indian for the requirements of tomorrow. I have described the Free Trader of the past, and now I propose to describe the Free Trader of today, and as he has been for the last two decades.

The building of the Canadian Pacific transcontinental road brought in its trail a class of very undesirable men. All rules have exceptions. I must therefore be just and not condemn all, but the majority of them were toughs and whiskey peddlers. They were the forerunners of the Free Traders of the present day, from Mattawa in the east to the shores of the Pacific on the west. They would start from some town back east with a keg of the strong alcohol, a few cheap gilt watches, some fancy ribbons, colored shawls and imitation meerschaum pipes, and if they found their bundles would bear a little more weight, they generally put in a little more "whiskey." They could almost always "dead-head" their way up the line on a construction train. Any place where they saw a few camps of Indians or half-breeds they dropped off with their stock in trade.

Such Indians as they found along the line were not hunters but they could act as guides to the Free Trader, and for a gaudy shawl or a few bottles of whiskey he could generally enlist one of them in his service. With an old canoe (furnished by the Indian) some flour, pork, tea and sugar, they could push their way up some river to a favorable point known by the Indian, and wait the canoes of trappers coming down on their way to one of the Hudson Bay posts at the mouth of the rivers.

The route of the railway cutting the large navigable rivers at right angles, at some parts of the line, as much as a couple of hundred miles inland of our posts gave the Free Traders a great advantage as they could intercept the Indians coming down from the height of land. Even to those Indians who had never tasted liquor the very word "fire-water" had a charm and an allurement not to be resisted. Probably the whiskey trader could keep the Indians camped at the place they first met for two or three days. Once he had got them to take the second glass he could name his own price for the vile liquor and put his own valuation on their furs.

I have heard of an Indian giving an otter skin for a bottle of whiskey. The skin was worth $15 and the whiskey possibly thirty cents. I knew positively of a trapper who gave a new overcoat worth $6 for a second glass of whiskey and when this took effect on his brain, for a third glass he gave a heavy Hudson Bay blanket that had cost him $8. The trader seeing he had nothing else worth depriving him of turned him out of doors on a bitter February morning.

Since these men have overrun the country the Hudson Bay Company has spent hundreds of thousands of dollars trying to protect the Indians against themselves. The laws of the Dominion are stringent enough as they are set down in the blue book of the Indian Department, but they are very seldom enforced. The difficulty is to get sufficient evidence to secure judgment or committal of the offender.

The Hudson Bay Company seeing the giving of liquor to Indians abased and impoverished him, abolished it by a law passed in committee in 1853. They saw that selling liquor to an Indian put him so much short of necessary articles to make a proper hunt, it weakened his constitution, laid the seeds of disease, and from a business point of view, was bad policy.

To make their posts perfectly free from liquor, the very yearly allowance to their officers, clerks and servants was discontinued and each employe was given the equivalent as a cash bonus at the end of each year. I must say a white man or two amongst a drunken band of Indians ran considerable risk; several have paid for their greed of gain with their lives. Amongst the Indians many lives have been sacrificed thru the liquor curse, shooting, stabbing and drowning being the principal results of their fatal debauches.

It is a most pitiful sight for one to travel on the C. P. U. line and see at the stations along the interior the ragged bodies and emaciated features of the Indians who hang about the stations. These are some of the good hunters of twenty-five years ago and their descendants. Back in those days an Indian's advances were only limited by his demands on the company. He took only what, under ordinary luck, he could pay for.

To-day hardly one of them can get trust for a dollar. They pass their summer hanging about the stations, the women doing a little fishing to keep body and soul together, and when the cold of winter drives them to the shelter of the forests, they have nothing necessary to prosecute a hunt even if they had the strength and energy to work. If one of their children or wives is lucky enough to trap an animal, the noble head of the family tramps off to the nearest Free Trader and barters it for tobacco and whiskey.

Coming back to the Free Traders I must mention the exception to the general run of them. In different parts of our territory organized parties of twos or fours have tried to oppose the company by trading in a straight way, that is, giving the Indian good, strong clothing and good provisions in exchange for his furs, but with very few exceptions the life of these small companies has been shortlived and I only know of one or two who made money by this trading.

The rock upon which they invariably come to grief is giving credit to Indians. A plausible story in the spring as to why they cannot pay is generally accepted by the Free Trader and a second outfit given the next autumn with the idea of enabling them to pay at the close of another hunting season. The Trader being called upon to pay up his supplies in either Montreal, Toronto or Winnipeg causes a sudden stoppage to their adventures and the field is open for some other party to go and have, most likely, the same disastrous ending.

No, I say it with unbiased mind that the opening up of the country to outsiders was a sorry day for the Indians. While they were dealt with exclusively by the Hudson Bay Company, they had the care and guidance of a parent, but the progress of settlement cannot be stayed and the end of the Indian is inevitable, and, like the buffalo, they will in a very few years be of the past.

The Great Company, who for two and a quarter centuries has been identified with the fur trade, is rapidly becoming a company of shopkeepers in the new towns and villages of the west. With the disappearance of the Indian will go the last of the class of men who caused his undoing, "The Free Trader."

CHAPTER III.

OUTFITTING INDIANS.

In these days of keen opposition it is only at the remote inland posts that we can supply the Indians with system; that is, as to amount of debt and a fixed time for sending them to the hunting grounds.

Taking Long Lake Post, north of Lake Superior, as a sample to illustrate our manner in rigging out hunters, I will say we appoint the 15th of September as the first day of supplies. On that day, early in the morning, the chief and his wife are called into the store, all others are excluded; this is done for two reasons — first, the Indian himself does not like the others to know what they take, or the amount of their debt; and, secondly, we find that when others, who are only onlookers are in the shop, they distract the attention of the Indian, who is taking the outfit and delay us in our work. The first thing done after the door is closed and locked is to talk over the pros and cons with the Indian as to where he is going to hunt, and his prospects, and from this an amount agreed upon as to the extent of his new debt.

This settled, we suggest that, first of all, necessary articles should be marked down; these we mention one by one and he replies if he has such already, good enough for another year, or if we are to mark down the article. The first essention, of course, is ammunition; so many pounds of shot and powder and so many boxes of percussion caps. Next on the list of his wants would be an axe, or axes, an ice chisel, steel traps, twine for a fish net, a few fish hooks, two or three mill-saw files (to sharpen his ice-chisel and axes) matches, a couple of bottles of pain-killer and the same of castor oil, and some thread and needles, (glovers and round).

Then comes the imported provisions. To an ordinary family of a man, his wife and two or three children, he will take 200 pounds flour, 50 pounds compound lard, 10 pounds tea, the same of tobacco, 2-pound cart of soda, 25 pounds sugar, another perhaps 12 or 15 pounds pork. This latter must be pure fat, meatless and boneless.

When we get this far in his supplies, a pause is called and he asks us to add up how much the foregoing comes to. Say this amounts to $100 and the amount agreed upon is $200, he thus understands he has $100 yet to get, or as much as whatever the balance may be. Then he begins over again by taking heavy Hudson's Bay blankets; these we keep in all sizes from one to cover an infant up to what we call four point, this latter is large enough for a double bed and big enough for the man and woman to tuck themselves comfortably in. Of blankets he may take two or three.

The next on the list is heavy strouds, blue for the woman and white for the man's leggings; following this will be a warm cloth skirt for his wife and enough Estoffe du pays for his pants a pair of ready made mole skin pants for ice walking during the excessive cold of January and February, several yards of English flannel, colors according to their taste; we keep in stock, white, crimson, yellow, sky blue, navy, and bright green; this is for underwear for the family, two pairs of heavy wool socks for the man and two pairs long wool for his wife. A half dozen red, spotted handkerchiefs, these are put to several usages, such as tying up the hair, as a muffler about the neck, tying up their little belongings and many other usages apart from what a white man would apply a handkerchief.

Several yards also are taken of a strong cotton for dress use, or outside skirts; this is imported by us direct and goes under the name of "Stripped Yarmouth Druggets." It is very durable and stands the rough wear and tear of the bush. Should his proposed hunting grounds be remote from a deer country he would take dressed leather for mits and moccasins, parchment deerskin for his snow shoes. Snow shoes, of course, each one of his family must have, and supplying himself with this leather, makes quite a hole in the amount of his debt.

Here again another addition of figures is made; perhaps a few dollars yet remain to complete the agreed upon sum. He and his wife, on the floor of the shop, handle each article they have received, and think their hardest to remember some forgotten necessary article that may have escaped their memory. We also, from long use to the Indian's requirements, come to their assistance and sometimes suggest something quite overlooked, but very necessary.

A further adding up is now made; they have positively all they require for the winter months, and yet a few dollars remain to make up the amount, and then the Indian's weakness shows itself and he says: "Oh! well give sugar and lard for the remainder." Then he and his wife make all the purchases up into one or two blankets; an order on the provision store is given him and his account is made up and given him in the following manner.

Pa-pa-nios, dr. to Hudson's Bay Co.

Long Lake Post.

X X X X X X X X X X

X X X X X X X X X X

Sept. 15, 1895

$200.00   M. H.

They don't generally understand figures, but they all understand that X stands for 10. As the Indian kills his furs, he adds them to his pack in saits often, at the same time scoring out one of the crosses on his debt slip. After all has been cancelled, he then hunts a few more skins to cover any misvaluation on his part, or to have something extra to barter for finery.

After the chief leaves the shop another man and wife are called in according to their standing in the band, and thus it goes on till we reach the last one. Six to eight families are about all we can get thru in a day, as there is so much time wasted in talk.

If we begin on the Monday, we generally see the grand departure take place on the following Saturday. We only import the best of everything and the Indian buying from our stores is assured of the purest provisions and the strongest and most durable goods. This is no boast for where we have no opposition the Indians and our interests are identical, and the company's agent at such posts has the Indians' welfare at heart.

On the frontier we are obliged by other buyers and circumstances over which we have no control to take common out of season skins. As the Indians find sale for skins of any kind, they hunt actually ten months out of the twelve. At our interior posts, where our word is law, we appoint the 25th of October to begin hunting and the 25th of May to finish; except for bears, and these they are allowed to hunt up to the 10th of June. What a sad sight it is for an officer coming from some interior district to a frontier post, where he left well-clothed contented Indians to find those swindled by the unprincipled traders, in rags, drunken and the seeds of consumption marked in their faces.

CHAPTER IV.

TRACKERS OF THE NORTH.

What appears marvelous and positively uncanny to a town person is simple to a bushman.

Years of continuous observation develops the bump of locality, every object has a place and meaning to a trapper; his eye is ever on the alert, and what his eye sees is photographed on the brain and remains there for future reference at any time he may require it.

This bump of locality is highly developed in all Indians and whites who have passed many years in the bush. Without the faculty of remembering objects a bushman could not find his way through the dense forests.

Providing the trapper has once passed from one place to another, he is pretty sure to find his way through the second time, even if years should have elapsed between the trips. Every object from start to finish is an index finger pointing out the right path. A sloping path, a leaning tree, a moss-covered rock, a slight elevation in land, a cut in the hills, the water in a creek, an odd-looking stone, a blasted tree — all help as guides as the observant trapper makes his way through a pathless forest.

Of course, this tax on the memory is not required of trappers about a settled part of the country, but I am telling of what is absolutely necessary for the safety of one's life in the faraway wilds of the North, where to lose one's self might possibly mean death.

I followed an Indian guide once over a trail of 280 miles, whereon we snowshoed over mountains, through dense bush, down rivers and over lakes. To test my powers of a retentive memory, the following winter, when dispatches again had to be taken to headquarters, I asked the Indian to allow me to act as guide, he following.

On that long journey of ten or twelve days, always walking and continually thinking out the road, I was in doubt only once. We were standing on the ice; a tongue of land stood out toward us; a bay on either side. The portage leaving the lake was at the bottom of one of these bays, but which? The Indian had halted almost on the tails of my snowshoes, and enjoyed my hesitation, but said nothing. To be assured of no mistake, I had to pass over the whole of last winter's trip in my mind's eye up to the point on which we stood. Once the retrospect caught up with us, there was no further trouble. Our route was down the left-hand bay.

When the Indian saw me start in that direction, he said: "A-a-ke-pu-ka-tan" ("Yes, yes, you are able").

The most difficult proposition to tackle is a black spruce swamp. The trees are mostly of a uniform size and height, the surface of the snow is perfectly level, and at times our route lies miles through such a country, and should there be a dull leaden sky or a gentle snow falling, there is nothing for the guide to depend on but his ability to walk straight.

It has been written time and again that the tendency when there are no land marks is to walk in a circle.

By constant practice, those who are brought up in the wilds acquire the ability to walk in a straight line. They begin by beating a trail from point to point on some long stretch of ice, and in the bush, where any tree or obstruction bars the way they make up for any deviation from the straight course by a give-and-take process, so that the general line of march is straight.

During forty years in the country, I never knew an Indian or white bushman to carry a compass. Apart from a black spruce swamp, it would be no use whatever.

In going from one place to another, the contour of the country has to be considered, and very frequently the "longest way round is the shortest way home." A ridge of mountains might lay between the place of starting and the objective point, and by making a detour round the spur of same, one would easier reach his destination, rather than to climb up one side and down the other.

On the first day after my arrival in London (the only time I ever crossed the water) a gentleman took me out to see some of the sights. He lived on the Surrey side, and took me direct, or, I should say crooked, into the city across the Thames. After walking me around several blocks and zigzagging considerably about, he came to a sudden stop at a corner. "Now," he said, "Hunter, suppose I was to disappear all at once, do you think you could find your way back to Elm Tree Lodge? I have always heard that you bushmen can find your way anywhere."

Now, although there was no necessity for it, my years of schooling had caused me to observe every conspicuous object, and every turn we had made since leaving his residence; and therefore I replied, with the utmost confidence, "Why, to return to your house from here is as simple as falling off a log."

Looking at me with the greatest incredulity, he said, "If you can find your way back unaided I will pay for the best hat in London."

"Well, my dear sir, my number is 7, and I want it soft felt and dark bottle green. Now follow me, and you can get the hat in the morning."

Without going into details, suffice it to say, I conducted him to his own door, and a more perplexed man was not in London; so much so, he had to call in his wife, his mother-in-law and his next door neighbor to tell them of my achievement.

At last I had to cut short his flow of words by saying my guiding him home was a most simple thing. It was merely the result of observing as I went along, and running the objects backward as I came to the house.

"If I was to tell you as a fact, my dear sir, that a bushman sees the track of some wild animal in the snow, he can tell you not only the name of the animal, but if it was male or female, within an hour of the time the tracks were made, if it was calm or blowing and the direction of the wind at that time and many other minor things, you would think this wonderful. Yet, as wonderful as this may appear, and hardly to be credited, an Indian boy of ten or twelve can read this page from nature as easy as one of us can read a page of print."

*   *   *   *   *

When the cold nights of the latter end of October had set in and the leaves were crisp underfoot, I decided to go and set up a line of marten traps through a stretch of green timber, between two large lakes. The distance was considered about eight miles.

I took an Indian youth as companion, for it is lonely work setting trap in the deep gloom of the forest alone. Our blankets, axes, two days' provisions, a square of cotton that we call a canopy, to keep off the wind, and my rifle, made up our necessary equipment, with a few baits to start work upon.

During the summer I had got an Indian to leave an old canoe on the shore of the big lake where we expected to come out; this would save our coming back on our tracks, as we could return by the canoe route, which was considerably longer, but much easier.

We worked away all the day we left the post, and when camping time came we found a pretty, sheltered place, the back of a large, flat-sided boulder. Ten feet in front of this lay a large fallen pine tree, against which we built our fire. Then we cut a lot of pitch pine dry wood in short lengths and split, ready to replenish the fire from time to time during the autumn night.

It is cheerful when one wakes during the night to have a bright blaze in a few moments.

The boy had worked pretty hard all day, and, after eating to repletion, rolled himself in his blanket and fell asleep. With me it was different. I lay back half-re-clining, half-sitting, enjoying the congenial heat and wondering what luck we would have from the traps when we made our first visit. My rifle lay alongside of me on the balsam brush, with the muzzle pointing toward the fire, and, uncon-sciously my hand grasped the stock and my fore finger toyed with the trigger. I mention all these details to show how easy what followed came to pass.

The sparks had all gone out of the wood and only a bright glow remained, enough, however, to light up the trunk of the pine log and a considerable distance each side of the fireplace. All at once I heard the crushing of dried leaves and the breaking of twigs, at some little distance off in the forest. The sounds were evi-dently made by some large animal, and I soon realized it was coming slowly with steady steps toward the camp.

My first thought was to chuck on some fresh fuel to scare whatever it was away; but the next moment I decided to keep quiet and await developments.

With my thumb I drew back the hammer of the rifle and waited. I kept my eyes steadfast in the direction whence the sounds came, and in a minute (it appeared an hour to me) I saw the head and forequarters of an immense black bear, which stood gazing down on the camp from behind the fallen tree.

To raise my rifle and sight it point blank at Bruin's chest was the work of an instant. Crash went the bullet, true to the mark, and the bear fell backward, making the woods echo with its death roars.

The boy sprang to his feet in a stupid, bewildered way, asking what was the matter. I did not take time to answer him, being occupied in getting a fresh shell into the barrel, for one never knows when a bear is really dead. The safest way is to have your gun ready and stand off at a reasonable distance and wait until he kicks himself stiff. In this case, however, it was soon over with its bearship, for the bullet had gone right through the heart.

The joy of the Indian boy knew no bounds when he saw the result of the shot, for he saw many gorges ahead of him.

I had always been led to believe that smoke, or the blaze from a camp-fire, would keep away the denizens of the Canadian forests, and when I told this bear adventure to old hunters they simply listened and gave a polite smile.

In this instance it must have been a case of inordinate curiosity, accounted for in a manner from the fact of its being a female bear.

CHAPTER V.

PROVISIONS FOR THE WILDERNESS.

All over the Hudson's Bay territory, in making trips, be it in winter or summer, there is a scale of provisions upon which a safe result can be assured. For each person of the party, per diem, the following is allowed, and that is multiplied by the supposed number of days that the trip is likely to last. Moreover, for each seven days calculated on, an extra full day's ration is thrown in, this is for safety in case of some unlooked for accident.

Provisions per man, per day: 2 pounds of flour (or 1½ pounds of sea biscuits), 1 pound of fat mess pork, 2 ounces of sugar, ½ ounce of tea, 2 ounces of peas (or same of barley), ½ ounce of carbonate of soda, and ½ ounce of salt.

The peas or barley are intended to be cooked during the night's encampment with any game the route may have produced through the day. With such rations I have traveled with large and small parties, sometimes with Indians only, and at others with Indian and Canadian voyagers mixed; have penetrated the wildest parts of two provinces, in canoes and on snowshoes, and was never short a meal. I admit that with the wasteful and improvident character of the Indians, the leader of the party must use due care and watchfulness over his outfit and see it is not wrongly used.

Take, for instance, the provisions for a party of seven men for fifteen days, the weight aggregates 347 pounds, and is of formidable bulk; and when the necessary camping paraphernalia, tents, blankets, kettles and frying pans, are piled on the beach alongside the eatables, the sight is something appalling, and the crew is apt to think what an unnecessary quantity of provisions; but before the journey is over we hear nothing about there being too much grub. Long hours, hard work and the keen, bracing atmosphere gives the men appetites that fairly astonish even themselves.

If a party is to return on the outgoing trail, and after being off a few days finds it is using within the scale of provisions, it is very easy to *cache* a portion for the home journey with a certainty of finding it "after many days," that is, if properly secured. If in the depth of winter, and there is a likelihood of wolves or wolverines coming that way, a good and safe way is to cut a hole in the ice some distance from the shore on some big lake, cutting almost through to the water. In this trench put what is required to be left behind, filling up with the chopped ice, tramp this well down, then pour several kettles of water on top. This freezes at once, making it as difficult to gnaw or scratch into as would be the side of an ironclad. I have come on such a *cache* after an absence of three weeks to find the droppings of wolves and foxes about, but the contents untouched. One could not help smiling on seeing these signs, imagining the profound thinking the animals must have exerted in trying to figure out a plan to reach the toothsome stuff under that hard, glazed surface.

At other seasons of the year a good *cache* is made by cutting and peeling a long live tamarac pole. Place this balanced over a strong crutch, tie what is to be left secure to the small end, over which place a birch bark covering to keep off the rain (or failing the proper place or season for getting bark, a very good protection is made with a thatch of balsam boughs placed symmetrically as shingles) and tying all in place, tip up the small end, weighting down the butt with heavy logs or stones; and possess your mind in peace.

Two of the best auxiliaries to a short supply of provisions that a party can take on any trip in the wilds of Ontario or Quebec, are gill-net and snaring wire. As food producers, I place these before a gun. Most of the interior lakes contain fish of some sort, and a successful haul one night can be smoke dried to last several days without spoiling, even in hot weather. So long as they are done up in a secure manner in birch bark to keep out blue flies, the greatest danger of their going bad is prevented.

Another very good way to preserve and utilize fish, is to scorch a small portion of flour (about one-third the quantity) and mix with pounded up, smoke dried fish, previously cleaned of bones. This makes a light and sustaining pemmican, easily warmed up in a frying-pan, and if a little fat can be added in the warming process, one can work on it as well as on a meat diet.

Admitting that there are years of plenty and years of scarcity with rabbits, there must be a dearth indeed when one or two cannot be snared in some creek bottom near the night's camp. A gun on the other hand may be only an incumbrance on a long journey. A chance shot may well repay the person carrying it, but very frequently a gun is quite useless.

We crossed the country some years ago between St. Maurice and Lake St. John. It was at the very best time of the year to see game, being in the month of May, when every living thing is full of life and moving about. The trip took us seven days going; coming back by another route we gained one day. On the whole of that journey through bush, lakes and rivers we only fired two cartridges, whereas our small gill-net gave us splendid fish each camping place.

Another trip I remember, this time in the winter, accompanying the men who carried the winter despatches between Pic River and Michipecoten, a distance of 120 miles each way. I was prevailed upon to take a rifle, as the route went over a very high mountain where deer (caribou) were seen every year by the men. Well, I suppose they told the truth; but I carried that gun 240 miles without firing a shot. No, as a possible help to stave off starvation, commend me to a net and snare in preference to a gun.

In my younger days in the Hudson's Bay Company's service I put in many years in what we call the Moose Belt in Quebec — that is, from the St. Maurice

River on the east to Lake Nipissing on the west from the Kepewa on the south to near the height of land on the north. All inside these boundaries was teeming with moose. They were killed in the most wanton manner by Algonquin Indians and the lumbermen, in many instances only the hide being taken, and the meat left. Our own Indians, who lived year in and year out in the country, never wasted a particle of meat. If they killed more than the family could consume during the winter months, before the warm days of April set in, it was carefully collected, cut in strips and smoke dried for summer use. While attending to the curing of the meat, the thrifty squaw dressed the hides. These were cut up and made into moccasins and traded at our store during their stay about the post in summer. An ordinary sized hide would cut up into about twenty-two pairs of shoes (without tops) and commanded $1.50 per pair, we selling them for the same price in cash to lumber concerns, making our profit on the goods bartered.

The young Indian the year prior to getting married always exerted himself to show how many moose he could kill. This was their boast and pride to show they were good providers of food. The Indian nature to kill would manifest itself at this time, and the numbers killed by some of the young slips is hardly to be credited. Older men with families never killed for the sake of killing.

I knew a young Indian personally whose mother had been left a widow with a large family. He was the eldest of the children, and that summer began to strut about the post in fine clothes and mix with the men of the tribe. This is one of the traits that shows itself before matrimony is contemplated. The killing of many moose was sure to follow these signs. That young boy actually killed to his own gun ninety moose. Averaging the butchered meat of each moose at the low estimate of 600 pounds, we have a gross weight of 54,000 pounds of good, wholesome food.

This section of country was in those days, I venture to say, the richest in game on the continent of America. Every little creek or lake had its beaver lodge, and even on the main routes of travel one would see beaver swimming two or three times in the course of a day's paddle.

At the posts we lived on fish, game and potatoes. Our allowance of flour was only 100 pounds for each man for the twelve months, and we used to spin this out by eating only a pancake or so on Sundays and a pudding on Christmas.

The choice bits of the moose — the tongue and muzzle — the Indians brought us in quantities, the trade price of each being half a "made beaver," equal to a supposed sum of fifty cents. This was paid in goods, and would be further reduced by 100 per cent, our advance for transport and profit.

One cannot but look back with regret to those days and think such slaughter was murder.

CHAPTER VI.
FORTS AND POSTS.

The Hudson's Bay Company's establishments comprised two Factories, several Forts and numerous posts, out-posts and smaller ones called "flying posts." I am writing of the days gone by for now, since the country is opened up, forts, as they were then known, no longer exist. The so-called factories were not places in which fabrics or other goods were manufactured, but more rightly speaking great depots where an entire year's supplies were stored in advance in case of a mishap to either of the ships.

The country was subdivided into the Northern Department and Southern Department. York Factory supplying the requirements of the former and Moose Factory the latter. At these places the summer months was their busy season, for not only did they receive the next year's outfit from the ships, but numerous brigades of boats and canoes were continually loading and departing for the far away inland posts and forts.

With the exception of one or two which were built of stone, the forts and posts were constructed of heavy hewn logs which, being placed flat to flat, were bolted with strong treenails every second or third tier until the desired height of wall was attained. The windows were mere narrow slits in the walls and as few as possible on the ground floor.

All the buildings were made in the same strong way and consisted, in an ordinary fort, of the master's house (or chief officer's dwelling); this was the most pretentious building in the lot, for not only did the factor and his family occupy it but it also lodged the clerks and other petty officials, besides furnishing a spacious mess or dining room and a guard room in which the officers lounged and smoked and the small arms were stacked ready for use.

Within the enclosure were the following other buildings, similar in construction to the great house. A store house in which was kept the bulk of the outfit and the furs gathered. A trade shop in which the Indians bartered their peltries. A men's house or servants' quarters. A work shop in which all necessary repairs were made on guns, harness, etc., and a stable to house the stock at night. They pastured, under guard, outside the walls during the day.

These buildings were generally in the form of a hollow square and the whole surrounded by a picket stockade ten or twelve feet high. This protection was made from trees of about seven inches in diameter, brought to a sharp point at the upper end and planted deep in the ground, touching one another. Here and there, inside, the stockade was reinforced by strong braces, which added to its solidity, should a combined force of men be brought against it.

At each of the four corners of the square a strong block tower was erected with embrasures cut therein for shooting from. In some of the larger forts small cannon were placed that commanded each side of the square and all around the inside of the pickets ran a raised platform on which men standing would be breast high to the top of the protection. This gave them a great advantage in shooting on coming enemies or repelling scalers.

Such places were only in the prairie country where the warlike and turbulent Black Feet, Bloods, Pegans and Sioux roamed. Amongst the bush or fish-eating tribes less severe precaution was required, altho the most of them were enclosed by the picket stockade and supplied liberally with muskets, cutlasses and side arms.

While the Indians were paying their semiannual trading visits the dwellers of the forts were confined pretty well indoors and the stock hobbled close to the stockades, for it was not always safe for a small party to be caught far afield. Great massive, barred gates opened into the fort, in the leaves of one side a wicket placed for the entrance and departure of men afoot, and it was thru this wicket an Indian and his wife were admitted with their furs to trade. When they were finished bartering and departed, two others were allowed in and so it went on.

The trade shop was so constructed that the Indian and his wife did their barter at the end of a long narrow passage, at the end of which a square hole was cut in the logs, behind which the trader stood with an assistant to fetch the goods required by the purchaser. The display of goods on the shelves was invisible to the Indian, but it was not necessary he should see them inasmuch as there being no great variety, everything being staple and the same from year to year, manufactured of the best material expressly for the Company.

The trade shop was always built near the gate and the guard at the wicket, after admitting the would-be purchaser of supplies, locked and barred the gate and conducted them to the entrance of the passageway along which all they had to do was to travel until they reached the trader at the end.

So that the Indian might know the amount of his means of trade the furs were taken in first and valued at a certain well-known currency of that particular part of the country in which he resided, i. e., "Made Beaver" or so many "Martens." In some places he was given the gross amount in certain quills and about the Bay in brass tokens. Of this latter coinage the Company had quarters, halves and whole M. B. (Made Beaver). Once this was mutually adjusted, trade commenced. The Indian would call for a gun and pay so many Made Beaver, a scalp knife, powder, shot and so on, paying for each article as he received it in either quills or tokens.

The outposts or "flying posts" were more in the bush country, where the Indians, as a rule, lived peaceably with one another and the whites. The smaller of these trading places were only kept open during the winter months and were generally built for the accommodation of the Indians and supplied with absolute necessities only. This enabled the hunter to keep closer to his work and not travel long distances, when furs were prime, for some positive requirement, such as the replacing of a broken gun. The keepers of these small posts were in most cases guides or deserving and trustworthy servants of long standing in the employ. With their families and a man or two they departed from the forts in September, taking the supply of trading stuff with them.

These small parties were self-sustaining, being given one day's provisions to take them away from the fort. After that until the next May they lived on fish and the small game of the country, with probably an odd wood caribou. The men of the party trapped furs while hunting game for their sustenance. The proceeds for the personal winter trapping of each servant was allowed him as a bonus over and above his wages. Cash was not given, but they had permission to barter the skins for what they chose out of the trade shop and they went principally in tobacco for the men and finery for the women.

Where fish and rabbits in their season was the mainstay with these people, prodigious numbers were required and consumed to sustain life. Thirty or forty white fish or the same of rabbits was an ordinary daily consumption of the dwellers at one of these "flying posts," but the reader must remember they had no auxiliaries to help out this plain straight food.

No butter, lard, pork, sugar or vegetables, just rabbit or white fish twice a day and nothing else. This was washed down with bouillon in which the food was cooked. Spring and fall they had a variety in ducks, geese, beaver and an occasional bear and then they lived in the tallest kind of clover while it lasted.

As no insurance company could be found who would take fire risks that could only be represented to them on paper by the interested parties, the Hudson's Bay Company began years ago to take certain sums of money out of each year's profits and created a marine and fire account, out of which fund any loss by sea or fire is met and the district or department where the accident occurred is recouped for its loss. Fires at the forts and posts have been of very rare occurrence, as the utmost care and precaution has ever been exercised in preventing such by the officer in charge.

Self-preservation is the first law of nature and the dwellers of these far away Hudson's Bay posts knew of no greater calamity than that of being burnt out and they looked to it that as far as precaution went this should not occur.

CHAPTER VII.

ABOUT INDIANS.

The way in which the Hudson's Bay Company managed the Indians of Canada has ever been admired by the people of the outside world. Their fundamental rule and strict order to their servants was never to break faith with an Indian. As time went on the Indians began to realize fully that the company was in the country for their mutual benefit, not as aggressors, land grabbers or people to take away their vested rights.

It soon became known that any promise made to them by a Hudson's Bay officer was as good as fulfilled. On the other hand, when "No" was said it meant No every time and there was never any vacillating policy. "Just and Firm" was the motto in all the Company's dealings with the natives and while they were at all times prepared, as far as they could be, to meet any trouble, yet they never provoked enmity. To do so would have been antagonistic to their interests even if justice and humanity were put aside.

Each officer of the posts had the welfare of the Indians as much at heart as a father has for his own children. In sickness they attended them, in trading they advised them what goods would be most beneficial and lasting to their requirements and as far as they could in a pacific way they advised them when trouble arose between any members of the tribe.

In those days when the Company had the country under their exclusive sway, no cheap, shoddy goods were imported in the trading forts. Durability was looked for, not flashy finery. These came with the opening of the country and the advent of peddlers and unprincipled traders. We see the results of this today at any of the stations where our transcontinental train stops. Bands of the once well-conditioned, well-clothed, sober Indians are now replaced by ragged, emaciated, vice marked descendants of these, hanging around in idleness, an object lesson of what so-called civilization has brought them to. Except in some far back isolated posts, the Indian's word goes for nothing. They have lost the once binding obligation that their promise carried and the trader can no longer depend on them.

As the writer knew the pagan and uncivilized Indian some forty years ago he was truthful, sober, honest and moral. I won't say the white man has willfully made him otherwise than what he was, but as a fact he is. It has been a transformation in which the Indian has fallen to most of the white man's vices and adopted very few of his virtues. My experience has been over considerable of the country and amongst several tribes and my observation has told me that about the Mission centers (be the denomination what it may) is to be found the greatest debauchery and rascality in the Indian and that right at their very gates.

Prior to 1821 both the Hudson's Bay Company and that of the Northwest gave liquor to the Indians, but after the coalition of the two companies a wise policy was inaugurated and liquor was stopped thruout the vast country. The Company's people saw that liquor to the Indian was laying the seeds of illness and death and impoverishing his family, but the Company did not take away the grog (which had been given in most cases as a bonus on their hunt) without giving an equivalent in value and the cash value of liquor to each hunter entitled to any was given in the shape of any goods he chose from the trade shop. Even the servants who had heretofore received a Saturday night allowance of spirits, received in lieu thereof two pounds sterling per annum added to their wages.

The Indian in the olden days seldom stayed about the posts longer than to barter his furs and got back to his hunting grounds with as little delay as possible. They were fish and flesh eaters, almost every river and lake abounded with the former and the surrounding woods furnished the latter and the Indian got his living from day to day with very little exertion. The Indian has no idea of hording up the treasures of this world and in only two instances did I know one to have a bank account. They have an implicit and abiding faith in kind providence to supply their wants as they go thru life and reason that what is sufficient for them will be forthcoming for their sons and daughters.

As an agriculturist the Indian is a failure. The life is too hard and humdrum for one whose ancestors from away back have lived a nomad life. His sphere of action on a farm is too circumspect and he pines and longs for the freedom of the wilds. It is a sad and not a successful measure, this corralling of the once lords of the country on restricted reservations which in plain English is no better than a prison to them.

The Indian in his native state is hospitable to a degree. The stranger who comes to his wigwam is given the best and choicest pieces of what his larder contains. The softest and best bed is made for him furtherest from the door. When he arrives no impertinent questions are asked as to his business, destination or his success in the hunt. Any such information that he thinks fit to impart is given voluntarily over a pipe of peace before rolling up in his robe or blanket.

It is not considered good form to ask questions, even a member of the family coming home at night is not asked as to what success he has had in the chase. His bundle or game bag is thrown inside the door and remains there until his mother has placed food before him. While partaking of this his mother (or wife if it happens to be the father) opens his bag and takes out, piece by piece, the contents. If he has killed a deer the head and heart only are brought to camp. If a bear, the four paws, if a moose, the tongue and muzzle.

The Indians are very superstitious as to how they treat the flesh and bones of the large game they kill. Beaver bones are never thrown to the dogs, but are carefully collected and sunk in the lake or river, thus returning them to the element from which they came. A bear killed by an Indian is always addressed as cousin and a harangue is given him by the hunter and his pardon asked for the necessity of taking his life. The bones, especially the skull, are hung up at the exact spot where he fell, journeys from camp often being taken with the express purpose of carrying out this sacred duty.

Deer and moose antlers and shoulder blades are generally found on stakes or dry knots of trees at the discharge of some big lake on main canoe route. There are certain parts of the flesh and insides of these animals that the women are never allowed to partake of, such as the head, heart and paws of the bear.

Likewise it is *infra dig.* for a man to carry water to the camp, chop wood or dry his own moccasins. After the killing of big game it rests with the women and children to cut up the meat and toboggan it to camp. The man merely walking ahead to show the way and lolling about an open fire while the work of butchering and loading sled is going on.

Physique and Health. — Before the Indian came in close contact with the whites he lived on the produce of the country and remained close to nature. He was of a wirey and healthy stature and lived to a ripe old age. Now from their acquired taste of the white man's foods, love of liquor, insufficient clothing and early marriages, the "white plague" has taken firm hold in every band and a few decades will see very few of the Government wards to be cared for.

How few of the thousands of immigrants now flowing into the country pause to consider that once these beautiful lakes, rivers, prairies and mountains were the resort and homes of a race of God's primitive children. Their wants were supplied with a lavish generosity by a Great Spirit and pagans tho they were said to be they cast their eyes heavenwards and thanked that Great Spirit for blessings received. And the translation after death that they looked forward to, to the Happy Hunting Grounds, what are these but our God and our Heaven?

Poor, fast disappearing race! I have lived with them, hunted with them and walked the long trail and from my city home I often yearn for the old life in that North Country.

CHAPTER VIII.
WHOLESOME FOODS.

Men are governed, or prejudiced very much for, or against, things by appearances or names. And this I find holds even with practical men as are hunters, traders and trappers, men who as a rule reason much, and are endowed with considerable common sense.

There are many food meats that the woods furnish that are tabooed from the hunter's bill of fare simply by the name of the animal that furnishes it. The skin is taken but the flesh is cast away, and this for no other reason but the name the beast is generally known under.

Take, for instance, the water rat, musquash, or the more generally used name of musk rat. Here we have certainly nothing against it but the name. Because did we of the fraternity of hunters pause to consider, and reason, we must see that a musquash ought not, and cannot be different from a beaver. They are identically the same in every detail except the formation of the tail. They live on the same food, roots, grasses, and twigs, as the beaver does and to the eye they are (barring the tail) a small beaver in miniature.

Musquash, like all animals in cold countries, are at their best condition in the autumn. Let my hunter friend take one of the above despised animals, select a nice mixed flesh and fat one, clean it as you would a beaver, split it up the front, impale it on a sharp pointed stick, introduce the point near the root of the tail, and bring it up to the inside of the head. Plant your screwer in front of your camp fire, giving it an occasional twist, while getting your tea and other things ready. When done stand it back from the excessive heat for a short while to cool and harden. Fill your pannican of tea, spread out your biscuits, cut off a quarter section of your roast suckling, and fall to, and a hundred to one you never ate anything more delicious. I know prejudice has to be gotten over, "I have been there myself."

I starved once for a day and a night, did hard paddling and portaging all day and went supperless at night, simply because I could not get over the idea of "rat." We had about a dozen with us, and my Indian companion roasted a couple each meal and demolished both himself with satisfaction and relish; for myself the thought of the name was enough.

Take again the Canadian lynx. Were this name always adhered to, there would be less room for prejudice, but unfortunately it is more frequently called cat. I admit it has all the appearances and manners of the cat, but let someone, unknown to you, fry some fat cutlets from the ham of a lynx, and fifty to one you will relish it as very fine veal and you cannot be convinced to the contrary. There again is the porcupine, I think sometimes known as the hedgehog. When they are in good condition, nicer or more juicy meat a hunter cannot put his teeth into. When properly prepared and properly cooked, the white mans "rarebit", the suckling pig, cannot prove its points.

The arctic or snow owl is a bird that gives as fine a flavored flesh, and the same in color and appearance as a fat capon. But where one is set against it, is when served up in Indian fashion, boiled whole, it has then the appearance of a young baby, and one would almost have to be a professional cannibal to tackle the object. The thick, plump thighs, the round bald head, makes the appearance to a young infant almost startling. However, if one closes his mental eyes to this similitude, the flesh is most toothsome.

I come now to another that occurs to me as being much despised, that is the festive and highly perfumed skunk. We look on a skunk, be it man or beast, as the meanest kind of thing, but I assure you the skunk (the four footed one) is not to be despised or cast aside when one is hungry or desires a change from the everlasting bacon and biscuit. A skunk, shot and prepared with care, makes very good eating.

Two of the animals of our forest I never could stomach and very few Indians eat them, be they ever so much pushed for food, and these are: the otter and mink. Their flesh is oily, black and highly flavored, resembling the meat of seal, only more so! The Indians as a rule look down with contempt on a fellow Indian who eats otter or mink, whether from necessity or from an acquired and perverse taste.

I venture to opine my little sketch will set many of my hunter friends thinking and perhaps make a few converts. You won't repent it.

*   *   *   *   *

Forty years ago, before the country was opened up to civilization and the usual provisions of the white man were imported into the wilds, the great staple foods of the territories, from the Labrador Atlantic seaboard to the Pacific, consisted of buffalo, caribou, white fish and rabbits. According to the parts of the country where these animals resorted, the Indians, traders and trappers, lived almost exclusively on their flesh, either in the fresh, dried or pemican state.

All foods, not imported, went under the name of country produce, and as flour is the staff of life to the white man, so was buffalo, caribou, rabbit or white fish to the dwellers of the north country. Beaver, partridge, porcupine and other small prey, a kind of entree, or side dish, got only at odd times, and not to be depended on for regular three times a day diet.

The quantity of any one of these four foods required to sustain, even a family of six, during a long northern winter, was something to make a layman incredulous.

The Indians living about the plains of the lower Saskatchewan and foothills of the Rockies not only lived on the buffalo, but made up immense quantities of pemican, which was parched in summer skin bags, weighing about sixty pounds each, and traded for ammunition, cloth, beads, hatchets, etc., at the forts.

From these bases of supply the bags of meat were sent to posts farther north, and used for tripping and feeding the men about the post. Large quantities were floated down each spring from Fort Ellis, Qu Appelli and other plain forts, by the Assiniboine to Fort Garry and from there in larger boats to Norway House, on Lake Winnipeg, which in those days was the receiving and distributing factory for all the country north and east, and had the distinction of being the place of council each year.

The people inhabiting the country embraced by the Mackenzie River, Great Bear Lake, and the coast of Lake Winnipeg, subsisted almost entirely on white fish. These were killed in great numbers each spawning season, not only for their own food, but for their team dogs as well, the posts putting past from ten to one hundred thousand, according to the importance of the place and the mouths to feed.

The fish were hung in number on skewers as taken from the water, the sharpened stake being run through the fish near the tail.

The string of ten fish on a skewer was called a "percer," and was hung head down from long horizontal poles, as high as a man could reach, and the length of these traverses would accommodate one hundred "percers." The great stock of fish was surrounded by a high picket stockade open to the weather, with one entrance, which was kept strictly under lock and key, and opened each evening by the post-master, i. e., steward, who gave out the requirements for the next twenty-four hours' consumption.

The expenditure was kept posted up each night, showing for what use the fish had been given out, under the following headings:

> Mess Account.
> Men's Rations.
> Indians visiting the post.
> Dog Rations.

Thus, at any time, the factor could tell the exact number of fish consumed and number yet on hand.

Many of the posts would have an expenditure of a thousand fish a week for all purposes, which would be about thirty thousand for the winter.

In the country lying south of Lake Winnipeg to Lake of the Woods and east as far as the Ottawa River, the staple food was the harmless little rabbit. It is a dispensation of Providence that the rabbit is a prolific animal, for they are the life not only of the people, but of martens, lynx, foxes, ermine, owls, hawks and ravens.

An ordinary family of Indians, living on plain boiled or roasted rabbits, require about twenty a day, and even that keeps their vitality a very little above zero. There is no doubt but what the food a man eats makes or lowers his valor and endurance.

No one ever heard of the fish or rabbit-eating Indians going on the war-path, while, on the other hand, the buffalo eaters were fearless men both as horsemen and fighters.

The Labrador Peninsula, bounded by the Saguenay river on the west, Hudson's Bay and Straits on the north, the Atlantic seaboard on the east, and the Gulf of St. Lawrence on the south, a country as large as England, France and Austria combined, is the home of the Caribou or wood deer, who migrate north and south in countless herds spring and autumn, and are followed by bands of roaming Indians continually preying on them.

As in the case of the pemican, these Nascapies, Montagnais, and Cree Indians bring into the posts dried meats, marrow fat and tongues to barter, and on this the post dwellers live.

With the Indians of the present day armed with modern rifles, and the great depletion in the calf-crop made by the marauding of wolves, the day cannot be far off that the caribou will be of the past as the buffalo is.

In their migrations north and south, at certain places well known to the natives, the deer have to cross rivers. Taking the crossings the mob of deer would compact itself so much that the traverse would be black with their bodies.

The Indians who had been waiting for some days the passing of the herd, would attack them from up and down the river in their canoes, shooting them with arrows, spearing and axing the poor frightened brutes in the water till the lower waters were covered with floating carcasses.

Much meat and many skins were spoiled for the want of quick attention. After the battle the Indians gorged themselves to such a state of repletion, that it rendered them unfit for exertion, but a just God frequently punished them during the bitter weather of the following winter by starvation, and whole families succumbed for want of the very food they so wantonly wasted in the autumn.

The Hudson's Bay Company had a post years ago on Lake Mis-a-ka-ma right on the tableland between Ungava bay and the Canadian Labrador coast, for the trading of deer skins, both dressed and in the parchment state. One year the skins were in such numbers that the boats of the brigade could not carry the whole to the coast, and bales of them had to be wintered over to the next year.

The Labrador has been for many years the base of supplies for fish and rabbit districts, where the natives have no deer to make moccasins, mitts and shirts, and the parchment for their snowshoe knitting.

These deer skins take a round about route to reach their destination, being in the first place shipped from Ungava, or Nigolette, to London, and after passing the winter in London, are reshipped to Montreal, via the St. Lawrence, and from that depot sent with the new outfit to posts that have requisitioned them the previous year.

One would think with the introduction of flour, pork and other imported provisions that the slaughter would be a thing of the past, but the killing goes on as before, and now only the skin is taken, the meat remaining to rot.

CHAPTER IX.

OFFICERS' ALLOWANCES.

To readers of H-T-T descriptions of modes of living in by-gone days will, no doubt, be as interesting as actual hunting or trapping. I therefore submit a reminiscence of days in the early sixties, gone never to return.

Transport then to the far inland posts was so tedious and costly that it was impossible to freight heavy stuff so far away, and the employees of the company had to live on what the company in which they were stationed produced. However, a scale of allowances of a few delicacies were allowed, and these were made up every year at the depot of each district, and were for one year. The laborers or common people about the post got nothing in the way of imported provisions, except when at the hard work of tripping. The officers' scale was as follows, be he a married man or a single man, it made no difference. Their several grades were as follows:

Chief Factor, Chief Trader, Chief Clerk, Apprentice Clerk, Post Master.

A Post Master did not mean a master of a post, but was generally a long service laborer, who could supervise the general work about the post and act as interpreter if required. He also received a minimum allowance from headquarters, but of fewer articles than that of clerks and officers. A Chief Factor, being of the highest grade in the service, received the largest allowance, which was as follows:

Three hundred pounds flour, 336 lbs. sugar, 18 lbs. black tea, 9 lbs. green tea, 42 lbs. raisins, 60 lbs. butter, 30 lbs. tallow candles, 3 lbs. mustard, 6¾ gal. port wine, 6¾ sherry wine, 3 gal. brandy.

Exactly one-half of the Factor's allowance was the share of the Chief Trader, and a half of the latter's portion was the scale for a Chief Clerk or Apprentice Clerk. A Post Master however, not receiving the full list, I will give in detail.

Fifty-six pounds sugar, 3 lbs. black tea, 1½ lbs. green tea, 7 lbs. rice, ½ lb. pepper, ¼ lb. pimento.

At every post where it was possible to grow potatoes they were given the greatest attention, as they constituted a very material place in the feeding of the post people. They were, however, kept under lock and key, and a weekly allowance given out by the Post Master. At posts where cattle were kept the allowance of butter was not supplied by headquarters, as we were supposed to make our own.

The allowances never came up with the general outfit, but were sent up in bulk to the headquarters of the district, and there parceled out for each post in that Factor's territory. The clerks or officers in charge of these out-posts went to headquarters about the 15th of August with a half-sized canoe. This being a special trip, made especially for the allowance of any small thing that might have been overlooked in the indent, was called "The Allowance Canoe."

A week was generally spent at headquarters in friendly intercourse with the staff there. The prospects for the ensuing year were talked over, and the requisition for the next year's outfit read carefully over, and any article requiring explanation or comment was then gone into by the Factor while he had the framer of the indent at hand.

This was the only time of the year that all the officers of that district met together, their respective posts being east, north and west, and hundreds of miles of forest and stream separating them. This reunion was a red letter week, and no sooner were we back to our posts but we looked forward to the next meeting. I doubt very much if today such a self-reliant, hardy and easily satisfied body of men could be found to fill similar circumstances.

It was etiquette not to arrive at headquarters before the date appointed. Occasionally a canoe from some post would have made extra good time coming out, probably gaining a day or part of a day, and would camp back of some point almost in sight of "The Fort." A noted last place of call before reaching the fort was called "Point a la Barbe."

Here a general clean-up took place, from a shave to clean linen and store clothes. As the lake upon which the fort is built was the main dropping-in thoroughfare from several parts of the interior, often two or three canoe parties would be at the "Point a la Barbe" at once.

A start would be made from there together, and when the rocky point which had hidden them from view was rounded a "flee de joie" was fired from each canoe, the paddle seized, and in unison with the quick stroke of the "paddle for the avenue," one of the usual French canoe songs was sung by the voices of the combined fleet till the rocky shores reproduced it from cliff to cliff.

Almost with the firing of the first shot the people at the post who were on the lookout ran up the glorious old Hudson's Bay flag to the flagstaff head, and an answering volley was returned. The handshaking, talk and laughter when the canoes beached was never to be forgotten.

Most of those at the fort had relatives or friends at one or other of the outposts, and if they were not present anxious inquiries were made and answered on the beach. Possibly some loved one had been called away since the last opportunity of communication with the fort; in such a case it devolved on some person of the new arrivals to break the sad news or receive bad tidings himself. In that case no words were necessary, the downcast look and the prolonged clasp of the hand told as well as words the bereavement. I have witnessed such meetings, and know it was only hours after the meeting that the details were imparted by words, and that night far into the small hours could be heard the death chant of the sorrowing relative.

Every night during our stay at headquarters our crews congregated at the men's guard room, and there hoed down the Red River Reels, and entered into other harmless pastimes till well up to midnight. During that week the former rigid discipline of the fort was considerably relaxed in honor of the strangers.

In the days of which I write liquor had been abolished for the servants and trade throughout the country, and a few years after even the officers' allowance of wine and brandy was cut off, so these dances were not attended by any discord or disturbance.

When the rum allowance was done away with to the servants, they received in lieu thereof two sterling per annum added to their wages, and to the Indian who had been in the habit of getting a gill of rum for every ten "made-beaver" traded, was given one skin for every ten traded, taking whatever he chose, to the amount of the aggregated skins, in goods.

For that one good deed alone, Sir George Simpson deserved the thanks of all throughout the territories when he abolished liquor as a stimulant to the men and a vehicle of trade with the natives.

The officers received no equivalent when their allowance was discontinued. It was brought about by the bad use one officer made of his allowance, and the others suffered thereby. A clerk's allowance of wine and brandy was done up in three oak kegs, each wine keg holding 2¼ gallons and the brandy one gallon. These were laced together with stout raw hide lashings, and the piece was called a "Maccrow," and a very awkward piece it was to portage.

The majority of the officers made it a point of honor to debark the Maccrow unbroached at their respective posts, and make the contents spin religiously through the next twelve months. Some could not withstand the temptation of sampling the liquor enroute, and had very little when they reached home.

It was one of these gentlemen who was the cause of the allowance being cut off. A petition was sent in to the Governor asking that we should receive the equivalent in money for the discontinuance of wine and brandy, which amounted to seventeen dollars at cost price, but no answer came, and we had to bear our loss and offer up some nightly words in favor (or otherwise) of the person who had made an abuse of his allowance.

CHAPTER X.

INLAND PACKS.

Prior to 1865, furs at inland posts were made up in packs of ninety pounds for transport to the frontier, but some of the young canoe men were not sufficiently strong to handle such a weight in debarking or loading them into the canoes, and a pack slipping from their grasp into the water and becoming wet inside caused delay to the whole brigade. A stop had to be made and the damaged pack unlaced, dried and repaired, before the journey could be resumed.

About the year mentioned, a top pack slipped off a man's back while being carried over a side portage, and before the man could save it had bounded down the hillside into the rapid, and was lost.

This happened to be a very valuable package, and its loss being reported called forth the next year, from headquarters, a general order to reduce the weight from ninety to eighty pounds per pack, and to make each package of pure skins — i. e., skins of only one kind.

This order to discontinue the mixing of skins was not pleasing to post managers, inasmuch as a smaller and better pack can be constructed of mixed skins than of only one kind.

For the information of trappers of to-day, I will give a summary of how many of each kind of skins made up, as nearly as possible, the prescribed weight of eighty pounds, thus:

> Forty large beavers and 20 small beavers made 80 pounds.
>
> Eight large bears and 4 small bears made 80 pounds.
>
> Five hundred spring rats, 80 pounds.
>
> Seven hundred and twenty large and small rats, fall, 80 pounds.
>
> Two beavers, large, for top and bottom covers, and 60 lynx skins made 80 pounds.
>
> Two beavers for covers and 30 otters made 80 pounds.
>
> Two beavers for covers and 50 fox skins made 80 pounds.

We had orders to gather such furs as fisher, ermine, wolf, wolverine, skunk, and any broken or damaged skins, and make up into a separate pack.

The fine and delicate skins, as marten, mink, silver and cross foxes, were to be packed in boxes thirty inches long by twenty inches square, and into this small compass the martens and mink, after being tied in bundles of ten skins each, were packed to the number of four hundred skins.

This made a very valuable package, and the greatest care was taken of it the whole journey. Valuing them at only $5 each, one of these boxes represented the sum of $2,000.

We all saw that this mode of packing would not last; as, taking the best of care, accidents will happen, and they began the very year after the order came in force. Leaving a disagreeable job to the last, the men at each carrying place avoided these boxes, and there was a struggle to see who would not carry them. The sharp corners abraded the men's backs, and when carried on top of a pack they hurt the back of the head; so, as a rule, they were generally left till the last load, and then taken with bitter comments, and a fervent wish that the promulgator of the order for such packages were himself present to portage them over the carry.

Two of these marten boxes were left by one of our crews in the middle of a brule. In making the former trip some careless fellow must have thrown down a half-burnt match; in a few moments dense clouds of smoke arose in their rear. The country was as dry as tinder, and in the space of a very few minutes the flames swept to the other end of the portage, licking up in passing those valuable boxes and contents.

We, figuratively, locked the door for the balance of that trip after the horse had been stolen, for the remaining boxes were stored each night in the officers' tent, and during the day a responsible person was on guard over them.

It was a severe loss out of the returns of one post. No one, perhaps, could be blamed for it, but it had the desired effect of repealing the order, and we were told to pack as in the good "old corn-meal days," and mix our furs.

To arrive at an average of each kind of skins through each and every pack, we counted the whole returns and estimated the gross weight, and then divided so many of each kind of furs through the several packs, something like this: 10 beavers, 2 bears, 40 marten, 10 mink, 100 rats, 4 foxes, 4 otters, 4 lynx — 80 pounds, or as the average might count out.

Previous to packing, the skins were neatly folded, placed in a pile and weighted down for a week. They were then built in the desired pack shape and underwent a severe wedge press hammering to reduce the bulk, then tied with three strong cross lashings, either of raw cowhide or twenty-four-thread cod line, and when all was secure, the wedges being released, the pack tumbled out complete, less the lateral tyings, which were two in number, of eighteen-thread cod line.

The size of one of these packs, ready for transportation, was 24 inches long, 17 inches broad, and 10 inches thick. The expansion of the compressed skins would, after a few days, give it a rounded shape in the middle, but when first out of the press it was almost perfectly square, and it was the pride of each post manager to outdo the others in the beauty and solidity of his packs.

A well-made pack would withstand the ill usage and the hundreds of handlings in making a journey of four or five hundred miles from an interior post, and would reach the first steamer or train of cars without a tying giving way. In my young days I have seen a pile of 296 of these packs on the beach at one portage.

An anecdote relating to the care of such a valuable cargo may be here appended. An old factor who had not left the interior for twenty-seven years, applied for and received leave to visit civilization with the understanding that he would take care of the furs in transit. This he did during a journey of days and weeks coming down the great river, standing at each portage till every pack was over, and checking them off by numbers and the aggregate.

At last he reached steamboat navigation, shipped his packs, and had the bill of lading in his pocket. Having shipped the furs he took passage on the same boat. During the midnight hours the captain, in making his rounds, was surprised to find a man sitting among the cargo. Who was this but Mr. S., still keeping his faithful watch. The captain asked why he was not abed in his stateroom.

"Well," he replied, "I saw rough deck hands going about the packs, and thought it better to keep an eye on them."

The captain laughed. "Why, man," he said, "we have signed bills of lading for those goods, and we are responsible for their safe delivery. Go to bed, Mr. S.," he continued, "and rest in peace, for even you have no right to touch one of those packs, now they are aboard this vessel."

That was in 1873, and I believe that old gentleman is alive yet. He retired many years ago and settled in Ontario.

CHAPTER XI.

INDIAN MODE OF HUNTING BEAVER.

Wa-sa-Kejic came over to the post early one October, and said his boy had cut his foot, and that he had no one to steer his canoe on a proposed beaver hunt. Now nice, fat beaver, just before the ice takes, is one of the tidbits that come to the trader's table, and having spare time just then I volunteered to accompany him, knowing I would get a share of the game.

As we made our way over the several small portages between the large lake on which the post is built and the one in which he had located the beaver, he told me there were two lodges on the lake to which we were making our way.

We pitched our tent on the last portage, so as not to make a fire near the beaver. Beavers have very poor eyesight, but very acute hearing and smell, and once they are frightened the sport for that night at all events is finished.

We had something to eat and then started for the lake, leaving our tent and things ready to return to after dark. Smoking and talking are forbidden when one is in a beaver lake; care also must be taken that the paddle does not rasp the side of the canoe.

The beavers had built an immense dam across the discharge of the lake, and left a small cut in the middle for the overflow to pass. Here Wa-sa-Kejic placed a No. 4 Newhouse trap in about 4 in. of water. On a twig 9 in. high and set back about a foot from the trap he placed a small piece of castorum. The smell of this attracts a beaver. Then he lengthened the trap chain with three strands of No. 9 twine, tying it to a stout pole, which he planted very, very securely in deep water, out from the dam.

The beaver, when he finds himself caught, springs backward into the deep water and dives to the bottom; here he struggled to get away until shortness of breath compels him to rise to the surface, and this is repeated until the weight of the trap is too much for his exhausted condition, and he died at the bottom, from whence he is hauled up by the hunter when next visiting his traps.

After placing the trap on the dam Wa-sa-Kejic opened another ready for setting, tied the poles, and had everything ready; then giving me implicit injunctions not to make the least noise, told me to steer the canoe quietly to the lodge, which was fixed in a small bay out in the lake. When we reached the beaver's house, he carefully placed the trap in the same depth of water as he had done the previous one, with this difference, that he omitted the castorum, because, as he told me afterward, the beavers went on top of the house every night, the young ones to slide down into the water, and the old ones to do any necessary plastering.

Another trap was set at the next house, and from there we paddled the canoe a considerable distance from the beaver works, and figuratively rested on our oars until sundown.

We were now going to try still-shooting them. Before night sets in about sundown each fine evening in the fall the beavers leave their lodge, first, to eat the young willows along the shore, and after satisfying their hunger to patch the dam, plaster their houses and cut young trees to store up for their next winter's food!

They come to the surface on leaving the lodge, and unless something frightens them swim on the surface in and out along the borders of the lake until they see a favorable spot to go ashore; and here they set to nibbling the bark of young birch or popular, and if the hunter is careful he may be shot at close range.

As I said before, talking while hunting beaver is forbidden; and the hunter conveys his wishes to the steersman by signs, thus: To draw his attention he oscillates the canoe slightly; to move the canoe ahead the motion of paddling made by throwing the opening hand inboard; to alter the course of the canoe is done by signing with the hand either to the right or to the left, as desired; to stop the canoe's headway when getting too close to the game is done by gentle downward patting of the hand, etc.

Being already versed in this dumb language, we shoved away and took up a position near the lodge, but to the leeward of it, and waited. The sun having already gone down behind the forest, on the other side of the lake, we had not long to wait until a beaver broke water and swam away in a direction from us. Wa-sa-Kejic shook his head, as much as to say, "We will go after that fellow later on." The first was followed quickly by a second, a third and a fourth! Then, after waiting for fully fifteen minutes and no other appearing, Wa-sa-Kejic made signs to go ahead; this we did slowly, without taking the sharp-bladed paddle from the water.

Presently we heard a noise as if a pig were supping up from a trough. This was one of the beavers crunching up young twigs in the water. The canoe was edged slowly toward the land, with Wa-sa-Kejic on the alert, both dogheads full-cocked and ready for action. Presently the downward motion of the hand was given, the gun brought deliberately up to the shoulder, and the next instant the explosion, followed almost as one shot by the second barrel! A thick smoke hung between us and the shore, but we could hear kicking and splashing of the water; that told the shot was true. The beaver had ceased to struggle by the time we reached the shore. "But for what was the other shot?" I asked Wa-sa-Kejic.

"For that," he answered, pointing to another beaver stone, dead on the bank; and then he laughed, for there was no necessity of keeping quiet any longer, for the shots had frightened any other beaver in the vicinity.

"We may as well go to camp now," continued Wa-sa-Kejic, "and we will see our traps in the morning."

From the fact of our having come ashore late, and perhaps more because of the hearty supper we made off of roast beaver, we did not awake until the sun was high. We immediately partook of a hasty breakfast of tea Gallette and pork and went to see the traps.

"Fortunate?" Well, yes! We found one in each trap; and returned during the afternoon to the post. The Indian gave me the meat of two beavers for myself.

He left his traps set to visit at some future time, because there were several animals yet in the lake. Describing the mode of killing beaver would not be complete unless we explained that of "trenching." This method of killing them is largely practiced by the Indians after the lakes and rivers are frozen over. I cannot do better than to describe a small lake that Wa-sa-Kejic and I went to trench in December. This beaver lodge I had found the very last day of open water, for that night the wind turned round north and froze up everything! As it was close to the post, and I had found it, I simply made a bargain with Wa-sa-Kejic to do the trenching for a pound of tea. In those days tea was tea in the remote interior, and meant many a cheering cup to the Indian.

Wa-sa-Kejic whistled his dogs after him when we left camp in the morning. The lake lay in the hollow of a mountain of considerable height, and could be compared to an inch of water in the bottom of a teacup. Before we were half down the precipitous sides we saw the dogs nosing around the shore, scenting for the beavers in their "washes" or breathing holes. Wa-sa-Kejic, when he cast his eye around the small body of water, said, "This is an easy lake, and the beaver will soon all be dead."

He now produced an ordinary socket chisel of 1½ in. point, and in a few minutes had this handled with a young tamarak about 6 ft. long. We each carried an axe, and the first order I got was to cut some dry sticks that stood at the discharge, each stick to be about 4 ft. long. These, as fast as cut, the Indian drove across the creek, after he had cut a trench in the thin ice from shore to shore. This was to prevent the beaver from going down the creek.

The next thing was to break open the lodge from the top. This was done to scare the beavers out into the lake and make them resort to the washes. The beaver washes have their entrances under water, and go up sometimes a considerable distance from the shore, terminating generally under the roots of a tree. The beavers flee from wash to wash, as the hunter finds them out, and as each wash is discovered by the dogs (which scent the beavers through the frozen surface) the hunter stakes up the entrance to prevent them from returning.

Beaver washes vary in number according to the formation of the lake, from two to three up to twenty. The practiced eye of the hunter tells him at once if the lake has few or many. And this is why Wa-sa-Kejic said we would soon kill the beaver. At last the three dogs remained pointing and listening about 12 ft from the shore under a spruce of considerable size. The Indian set to work to stake up the entrance, which he did as fast as I could furnish the sticks.

On the shore of this barricade he cleared away the ice and snow, making an opening about the size of a barrel head, and then he paused, and pointing to the water, said, "See that! That's the beaver breathing!" This was shown by the water's surface gently rising and falling.

He now took off his coat, and baring his right arm up to the shoulder he gave me the ice chisel and told me to pierce the ground where the dogs were pointing. I had hardly given a blow or two before I saw Wa-sa-Kejic stoop over the hole and plunge his naked arm into the water. Instantly it was withdrawn, and a big fat beaver, securely seized by the tail, was struggling in his grasp. A blow of his axe on the spine finished him in quick order, and this was repeated from time to time as I continued to enlarge the hole where the beavers were huddled together under the roots.

We got six out of this wash, and two out of another, which constituted all that were in the lake. Two each made a very good load for us going home, and the next day I sent a man with a flat sled to bring home the remaining four.

The three principal modes of killing beavers are by shooting, trapping, trenching.

*   *   *   *   *

As a haunt and home of the muskrat, I venture to say that Cumberland, on the Saskatchewan, is the banner producing post on this continent. For miles and miles about this trading place there are immense grassy marshes, cut up and intersected by waterways and lagoons in every direction. From a hundred to a hundred and fifty thousand musquash skins was the usual returns from the post a few years ago. Three times during the year the hunters made their harvest, first in October, when the little animals were busy making their funny little cone mud houses and cutting bunches of long grass for their winter's food.

At that time the Indian would set his bunch of No. 1 steel traps before sundown and then lay off in his canoe at a short distance from the shore in some pond and shoot at those swimming past until it became too dusk to fire. Then he would make to some place to dry ground, haul up his canoe, make a fire and have his supper. When his after-meal pipe was finished he would silently shove his canoe into the water and make his first visit. When setting his traps he would take the precaution to place on the end of the pole that the chain was fastened to, a piece of paper, a bunch of grass or a piece of birch bark. This enabled him to find his traps in the dark, as the sign would show on the sky line as he paddled slowly along sitting low down in his canoe. The looking at his traps and resetting of them would take him an hour or two, then he would come back to his fire place, throw the rats he had caught in a pile, replenish the fire and stretch out for another smoke. About ten o'clock he would make another visit and on his return make a lasting fire, roll himself in his Hudson's Bay blanket and sleep till morning.

Often two visits were made in the morning, one just at the screech of day, and the last one after he had had his breakfast. Traps were taken up at this first visit to be set in some other locality that afternoon, and the hunter would paddle away for his lodge, where he would sleep all the forenoon while his wife and children were skinning and stretching the pelts. The next and every night would be spent in the same way until the ice took, and then another mode of sport I wish to describe would take place.

Ice in one night on these shallow waters was sufficiently strong to support the weight of one man. Armed with a long barbed spear a couple of feet in length, lashed to a stout pole, a bag on his back to put the rats in, and sometimes followed by a boy at a distance, the Indian, with his bright steel skates firmly buckled on, would glide down and in and out these skate lanes looking for rat houses. Practice and experience taught him to get over the ice in the least noisy way. Instead of striking out one foot after the other, he skated as the people of Holland do by a motion of the hips. It is not a graceful way, but it is easy on the skater of long distances on new glare ice. Sliding, as it were, down to one of the mud cones with spear firmly grasped, he would drive it down into the center, and very rarely missed transfixing one and at times two of the highly perfumed little animals.

The interior of a rat house is a saucer-like hollow in the center, just a little above the level of the water. From the edge of this there may be three or four slideways into deep water. At the least alarm the rats tumble down these in a minute and only return when all danger is past. When the inhabitants of a single house number eight, ten or twelve and they huddle together for warmth, they are often one on top of another, and thus the spear passes thru two at one thrust. The yet unfrozen mud is torn away and the spear with the rats lifted out, dispatched and placed in the bag, and the hunter bears down to another house and so on thru the day. When the bag becomes too heavy it is emptied out on the ice and the hunt continued. Towards night the Indian retraces his road and picks up the piles he left earlier in the day. His leather bag is converted into a sled, the ends of his long waisted sash are tied to the bag, and with the loop over his shoulder he strikes out a road straight for his camp, well pleased with his day's sport and himself. Knowledge of the architecture of the musquash's house (for they are all modeled in the same way) enables a bush man to know just where the little family are huddled.

There is yet another way numbers are killed just after the ice takes, and before the mud houses become too hard frozen; that is to skate down on them shot gun in hand and fire right into the cone of mud. The effect is not known till the earth is pulled away. The shot being fired at such close range there is, not unfrequently, three or four dead rats. One can not help to moralize how cruel it is for man to destroy at a moment the labors of long nights of these industrious little animals, and cause the remaining one to patch up the break at a season when it can never be as good and warm as when the work is done during open weather.

The hunter therefore sets his traps, so as to keep them employed, but he kills the greater number with his gun. A very small charge of powder and shot is required, and if the hunter keeps perfectly quiet in his canoe, and is below the wind, he can call the rat to within ten feet of his gun. I have pushed by canoe out from the shore of a small lake and called, just about sundown, and have counted no fewer than six rats coming from as many different directions. One waits till they get so close that they sheer off, and then fire sideways at the head.

CHAPTER XII.

INDIAN MODE OF HUNTING LYNX AND MARTEN.

Snaring is the principal way in which the lynxes are killed by the North American Indians. After a heavy fall of snow, however, if an Indian crosses a fresh lynx track, he immediately gives chase, even if he has only his belt axe.

The hunter only follows very fresh tracks, and in a short time comes up with the big cat. As soon as the animal knows it is pursued, it either climbs a tree or crouches under some thick shrub. If the hunter finds it up a tree, he sets to work at once to cut down the tree (that is if he has no gun). As soon as the tree totters he makes his way in the direction which it is to fall. The lynx clings to the tree until near the ground, and then springs clear. While he is floundering in the snow, the Indian bravely runs in and knocks him with his axe. Of course, if he has his gun, he simply shoots the cat and it tumbles dead to the foot of the tree. The feat of running down a lynx and shooting him with a bow and arrow is what all Indian youths aim to accomplish; they are then considered hunters.

Lynxes are always found in greatest numbers where their natural food supply is most plentiful. They feed usually on rabbits and partridges, and these are to be found in young growth of such trees as pitch pine, birch and poplar.

The Indian also, when he is dependent on rabbits, lives on the border of such a country, and has long lines of snares which he visits two or three times a week. Along this snare road at certain distances he has his lynx snares, which are nothing different from those set for rabbits, except being much larger. Yes, there is another difference: Instead of the snare being tied to a tossing pole, it is simply tied to a stout birch stick, 3 or 4 feet long by about 2 inches in diameter. The extreme ends of this are lodged on two forked sticks, and the snare hanging down in the middle is then set, tied to small dry twigs on each side to keep it in position.

At the back of the snare, at about 2 or 3 feet, the head and stuffed skin of a rabbit is fixed under some brush. The skin is filled with moss, or pine brush, and is fixed so as to look as much as possible like a live rabbit in its form. The head being to the skin gives it the natural shape and smell, and the lynx, walking leisurely along the snowshoe track, notices the game and makes a spring for it through the snare. In his headlong bound he carries snare and cross stick along with him, and as soon as he feels the cord tightening about his neck he not infrequently becomes his own executioner by getting his forefeet on the stick and pulling backwards as hard as he can. The more he struggles, the madder he gets, and pulls the harder to free himself, but this is, on the contrary, only making matters worse. The loop of the noose gets matted into the soft, thick hair of the throat, and there is no "slack" after that; in a few moments the great cat is dead.

Sometimes the lynx carries the cross stick in his mouth and climbs a tree. This is invariably the last tree he ever climbs, because once up the tree he lets the stick drop and it hangs down, generally on the opposite side of the limb from that on which the lynx is. As the cat goes down the tree on one side, the cross stick goes up toward the limb on the other and gets fixed in the crotch. As soon as the cord tightens about his neck he tries the harder to get down, and is consequently hanging himself.

Lynxes are very stupid. They will even put their foot into an open and exposed steel trap; and the better-off Indians often use small No. 1 traps instead of snares. This, however is only done latterly, and by the very well-off Indians. As a rule Indians only have traps for beaver, otter, fox and bear.

Lynxes are very rarely seen in summer, keeping close to the thickest bush. In any case, the skin is then of no value, and they are far from being "a thing of beauty," with nothing but a bare skin.

In the prime state they are largely used on the continent as linings, and each skin is worth about $4.

*   *   *   *   *

There are three kinds or qualities of martens recognized by the trappers.

First. — The pine marten that is found in the country covered by soft woods, such as pine, spruce, white fir and birch. This is the most numerous and consequently the skins are of least value. They are of yellowish brown color on the back and orange on the throat, changing down to pale yellow or white on the belly.

Second. — The rock marten; this is found in a country with stunted growth of spruce timber, a very mountainous district, the chief features of which are great crevices and boulders. Some of the skins of this variety are of great beauty, being dark on back, and throat and sides of gray or stone color.

The third kind, which is the scarcest, and consequently of most value, is the marten found in the black spruce country, or swamps of northern Labrador. The fur of this variety is of a deep brown color throughout the pelt, and at times the tips of the hairs on the rump are silver gray or golden brown. The latter are very rare, and such skins have been sold in the London fur market for £5 a piece! They are also much larger than the other kinds, the skins of the male often being from 24 to 30 inches long, exclusive of the tail.

The proper and most successful time for hunting is in the latter days of November and the whole month of December. They are hunted again in March, but by that time the sun has bleached out the color of the hair, which causes a depreciation in value.

As a business, trapping is the only mode of killing martens. They are rarely seen to be shot at, as they pass the days in thickets or hollow stumps, only emerging after nightfall to hunt their food, which consists of mice, birds, young partridges, etc.

Wooden traps are made in the well-known "figure-of-four" shape, and are set either on stumps or on the snow, flattened down with the snowshoes, and the trap built thereon.

It is considered a very good day's work in December for a trapper to construct, bait and set up twenty-five such traps. A real marten hunter (nothing to do with my name) camps each night at the end of his day's work until he has from 150 to 200 traps set! He generally visits them once in ten days or a fortnight, and if the catch averages one marten to ten traps it is considered very fair.

It takes the hunter two full days to rebait, clean out and freshen up such a line. When small steel traps are used instead of the deadfall, the hunter can cover more ground in a day and do better work than by making all wood traps. The steel traps are much more fortunate than the wood ones. In the "figure-of-four" traps, before the animal is caught it must seize the bait with its teeth and pull strong enough to set off the trap, whereas with the steel trap the mere fact of his coming to the doorway to smell insures his putting his foot in it, and in a moment up hangs Mr. Marten or Mr. Mink, as the case may be!

Of course the steel traps have this disadvantage — they are weighty; that is, when you have fifty and over on your back, but the man who follows trapping as a business can very easily overcome this difficulty by placing catches of traps at different places by canoe near where he proposes to have his line in the winter; and he can then branch off now and again for a new supply as he is setting up his trap road.

This leaving the main road at right angles once in a while might even be a source of profit to the trapper, for he might come across a bear den or a beaver lodge, or fall on deer tracks, and if he succeeded in killing a deer some of the sinewy parts would come in to bait his traps.

The taking of the skins of these little animals is very simple. The knife is used only about the head; once back of the ears the skin is drawn steadily until the tail is reached, the core of which is drawn out, either by a split stick or by the stiff thumb nail of the trapper. The skin is then dried on flat (three) splints, and when dried sufficiently to prevent it spoiling is tied up with others to the number of ten in each bundle, and are thus taken to the trader or fur dealer.

The first purchaser from the trapper generally buys them at an average price, but he sells them to the manufacturer selected; that is, getting a high price for the dark and a low price for the yellow or pale.

CHAPTER XIII.

INDIAN MODES OF HUNTING FOXES.

The fox as a rule is a most wily animal, and numerous are the stories of his cunning toward the Indian hunter with his steel traps.

Starvation makes them catch in deadfalls, but they must be very starved indeed before they pull a piece of frozen bait and have a weight fall on their back. The skins of foxes killed during starvation are never so valuable, as the hair then lacks the rich gloss. When small game is plenty, such as rabbits and partridges, and foxes are few, the skins are of a deep richness not seen under other circumstances.

There are several different and distinct colors of foxes of the north country. They are all of the same family, with the single exception of the white or arctic fox. These, apart from their difference of color, differ very much in their characteristics. They are not cunning; on the contrary, they are positively stupid. They will readily catch in deadfalls, and will walk into an open, uncovered steel trap in daylight! Again the flesh of the arctic fox is eaten as readily as that of the hare or white partridge; all other foxes are carrion; even a starving Indian would give them the go-by.

Of the other or true fox we have many colors and shades of color, and I give them in their cash value rotation, beginning with the black or pole fox; First, black or pole; second, black silver; third, silver gray; fourth, black cross; fifth, dark cross; sixth, ordinary cross; seventh, light cross; eighth, dark blue (i. e., lead color); ninth, light blue; tenth, bright red; eleventh, light red; twelfth, arctic white; thirteenth, pale red.

Number thirteen is the poorest quantity of the fox family, and is worth less than the arctic white fox.

January is the best month for trapping. First, because the fur is then at its primest, and second, food is harder to get and the fox consequently more likely to enter a trap.

Of course, any number of traps will catch a fox, but not every trap will hold him. There is such a thing as the trap being too large and strong, as well as too small and weak! When too large and strong it catches too high up the leg, and being too strong it breaks the bone at the same time; and then in cold weather it's only a question of a few minutes for the frozen skin and muscles of the leg to be twisted off and Master Fox runs away on three legs, ever after to be too cunning to be caught in a trap. On the other hand, if the trap is too small and weak it catches the fox by the toes, and he either pulls his foot clear at once or the toes, becoming frozen and insensible to feeling, are twisted off; and this, if anything, is a harder fox to circumvent than the one with half a leg.

The proper trap to use is a Newhouse No. 2. When properly set it catches just above all the fingers, as it were, or where the paw or foot would correspond with the thick part of the hand. There is a good, solid hold of muscles, sinews, etc. There, once the jaws are fixed, they hold the fox to the death.

Fox hunters are very particular to keep everything connected with the trapping away from the house or camp, even wearing an outside pair of moccasins, which are peeled off and hung up with the snowshoes.

The hunter generally places his trap or traps on some bare point jutting out into the lake, or some narrows, or near a clump of willows at the edge of barren grounds, or any other place his judgment tells him a fox is likely to pass. The fewer signs the better; therefore instead of the chain being tied to a picket, a stick 4 or 5 ft. long is slipped through the ring on the chain up to the middle. Here it is securely fastened, so that it won't slip either way. A trench the length of the stick is cut down in the snow with the head of the axe, and the pole laid therein about a foot beneath the surface. Snow is then piled in and the whole packed hard.

The trap is now opened, and the snow packed down with the back of the man's mitt, large enough to lay the trap and spring therein. The trap is now open and about 2 in. lower than the surrounding snow. The hunter now begins carefully to lay fine flat balsam bows or clusters of needles from the palate out to the jaws until the whole is covered; then very gently he either dusts light snow over this until it has the same appearance as the rest or he takes up two large pieces of frozen snow and rubs them together over the trap until all is covered.

Chopped up frozen meat or fish, a supply of which the trapper is provided with, is now sprinkled or thrown about, beginning 15 or 20 ft. off and gradually getting more plentiful as the trap is neared.

With a brush broom the hunter dusts his snowshoe tracks full as he recedes from the trap until he is off 30 or 40 ft.; after that no further precaution is necessary for an ordinary fox. But for an extraordinary one I could relate a hundred different ways of setting traps and bait to overreach the wily old fellow; but in most cases it is time wasted, the fox eating the bait and turning the traps over night after night, much to the vexation of the hunter.

It is a pretty sight to see a black or silver gray fox jumping in a trap on the pure white snow. I went one time with Wa-sa-Kejic to see his traps in the barren grounds back of the post. I was following in his snowshoe tracks steadily, and we were just topping a small swell in the country, here and there clumps of black willows. All at once he stopped so suddenly in his tracks that I fell up against him.

"There," he said, "look at that!" My eye followed his finger, and there, jumping and struggling to get away, was a large black fox!

"Let me shoot him," I exclaimed, drawing my gun cover as I spoke.

"Oh, no," he replied, "we will only do that if he pulls himself clear of the trap."

And with that he drew his belt axe and walked with a steady step down on the fox. The closer he got the more the fox struggled, but he was well and freshly caught, and the trap held him fast.

Wa-sa-Kejic gave him a tap on the nose with the helve of the axe, which had the effect of stunning him. The Indian then seized him with his left hand by the throat, and with his right hand felt for his heart; this he drew gradually down toward the stomach until the heart strings gave way; there was a quiver, and the fox was thrown down on the snow limp and dead.

What a pleased look the Indian wore as he stood there, evidently oblivious to my presence for the moment, as he gazed down on the most valuable skin it was possible for him to trap. What a number of necessaries and luxuries this would procure for his family. He would get from the factor at the post $80 for that one single skin! What a number of any other skins it would take to amount to that sum!

CHAPTER XIV.

INDIAN MODES OF HUNTING OTTER AND MUSQUASH.

With steel or wooden traps is the only systematical way of hunting these animals. They are, of course, hunted for their pelts in the north country of Canada, and not for sport, as in Scotland. A few are shot, but these are met with by chance.

November is when the Indian sets his traps for otters. They have then their full winter coats on; and it is just before the small lakes and rivers set fast.

Their resort is generally in some chain of small lakes with creeks connecting the chain, and their home, if they can find one, is an empty beaver lodge. They prefer such a place, as after the ice is taken in fishing along shore, they carry the fish into one of the "washes," where they can breathe and eat with safety and comfort.

The otter is a great enemy of the beaver, but never willingly courts an encounter; yet, every time they meet, there is a terrible battle. I remember years ago coming out on a small lake about sundown, and seeing a great commotion on the surface of the water a few hundred yards out, jumped into my canoe and quietly paddled out. As I drew near, I noticed two black objects engaged in a deadly conflict. Although they must have observed the canoe, they paid no attention, but continued the fight, sometimes disappearing beneath the surface, fast to each other, for a full minute.

When within gunshot, I made out the combatants to be an otter and a beaver, and could have despatched the two with one shot, only I could plainly see they were both very much exhausted, and I wished to see which would gain the day.

The end was nearer than I expected. Once more they disappeared beneath the waters, each maintaining the same deadly grip of the other's neck; a few moments later the beaver floated to the surface on its back, dead. I looked about for the otter, and saw him swimming toward the shore, bleeding profusely from many wounds and evidently hurt to the death. I followed, however, with my gun full cocked, ready if need be to shoot him; but the beaver's long, sharp, spade-like teeth had done their work well, for the otter all at once rose half out of the water, pawed about for a minute in a blind way, turned over on his side, gave one convulsive quiver, and he also was dead.

A No. 3 Newhouse trap is generally used. In fact, this number is called throughout the country "otter trap." These traps are set at the overflow of beaver dams and otter slideways during the open water and at little portages used by water rats crossing from one bend of a small river to another. No bait is used; the trap is set in about 4 inches of water with a picket out in deep water to tie the chain to and a small piece of castorum on a forked stick.

The odor of the beaver castor has a very alluring effect on most all animals, and is greatly used by the hunter.

Traps for otters are set in the following way, under the ice: A place is selected in some small creek, connecting two lakes, where signs of otters are found. These signs are noticeable at the discharge of the lake, where the lake ice thins off into open water, for the ice is so thin that the otter readily breaks a hole to come out on the ice to eat the fish. The otter is a fish-eating animal, and is very expert in catching them.

Their slideways are generally made on some moss-covered, rocky promontory, jutting out into a lake. Here they will climb up one side and slide down the other for hours at a time.

Otters, when taken young, are readily tamed and become great pets.

Another way of setting traps in winter is under the ice in some creek where otters are known to resort. The ice is cut away from the bank, outward, for about 3 feet long by 1 foot or so wide. Each side of this cut is staked with dry sticks, driven into the mud or sandy bottom. The trap is set between the stakes at the outer end, in about 4 inches of water at least; that is, the water may be deeper than that, but two cross sticks are so placed that the otter in entering must go under the sticks and thus gets caught. The picket to secure the trap chain to is out from the trap, as in open-water time.

To induce him to enter, a small whitefish or trout is placed on a forked stick near the shore, and is so fixed that it appears to be alive and swimming. As soon as the trap is struck, the otter jumps backward into deep water, and for want of air is soon dead.

*　　　*　　　*　　　*　　　*

In Canada and the United States, the killing of the little animal known under the several names of water rat, musquash and muskrat is so well understood by the average frontier boy that any information I can give would be perhaps a repetition.

Still there is one way that the Indian practices which is certainly not known to the whites, and is at a certain time very successful. That is spearing them on the ice; and another mode in which the Indians are very successful in the fall is digging them out, or "trenching" them, in the same way they do the beaver, only with much less labor, as it is done before the ponds and creeks freeze up. I will describe the latter way first, seeing it comes before that of spearing.

The resort of musquash (always where they are in numbers) is along grassy rivers, creeks, or ponds; for they store up large quantities of the long, flat grass for winter use, as the beaver does with young birch and poplar. The Indian paddling along the shores of such places has his eyes fixed on the bottom of the water; presently he perceives the entrance to one of the rat burrows; he stops his canoe and gazes fixedly on the opening, which is always about a foot under water. At last he sees the water ebb and flow in and out of the hole. This is a sure sign that the "wash" is occupied at that very moment by one or more rats.

He at once, either with his axe or the blade of his sharp maple paddle, chops down the mud bank until he has an embankment or dam. This is to prevent the musquash from running out to deep water. When all is ready, either his wife or the boy who is steering the canoe is sent ashore to prod about the honey-combed bank with the handle of his paddle. The little animals thus disturbed and thoroughly frightened make a rush for the outlet, deep water and safety, but (there is always a "but") the Indian, with his upraised paddle, has his eye steadily fixed on the water back of his dam, and as fast as one makes its appearance the sharp edge of the paddle is brought down on its head or back, and it is thrown into the canoe, quivering in its death agony. From two to eight or nine are not infrequently taken from one hole. When the last one is killed, the Indian moves his canoe on until he finds another colony, and the same process is gone over again, and he returns to his camp with his canoe filled with musquash. I have in the fall received from one Indian as many as 2,000 skins, large and small.

Musquash breed twice in the summer, and bring forth at each litter from six to eight. In the fall the large ones fetch the hunters ten cents, and the kits, or small ones, five cents.

The spearing of the musquash is done in this wise: The rats throw up little mud-cone lodges, or houses, out from the shore, in about a foot of water. They are not unlike beaver lodges. The inside is hollow and the entrance is under water. In this resort the rats sit, huddled together, during most of the severe winter weather. The hunter, therefore, as soon as the ice will bear his weight, slides up to the rat houses, armed with a sharp, barbed, steel spear, about a foot long, let into the end of a small tamarac handle. This handle is generally about 8 feet long. Arriving close to the lodge, he poises the spear in mid-air for a moment and drives it down through the lodge with all his might. If he pierced a rat, he feels it wriggling on the spear, and keeps it fast there until he has torn away the mud and grass. He then seizes it by the tail and draws it with a jerk from the spear and knocks it on the ice, which finishes Mr. Rat. At times, when there are a number of musquash in the same lodge at the same time, the spear often passes through two, or even three, at one stroke. This is great sport where the lodges are numerous.

Musquash killed under the ice are worth two or three cents each more than in the fall, and the hunter makes frequently two to four dollars a day while it lasts.

The flesh of musquash killed under the ice is highly esteemed by the Indians. It has then its winter fat on, and is free from the objectionable odor which prevails in the spring.

The skins of the large ones, when dressed, make strong and durable lining for cloaks, coats, etc., and are made up into caps also. The "kit skins" are used in large numbers in the manufacture of kid gloves. The Hudson Bay Company exports annually about 3,000,000 skins.

CHAPTER XV.
REMARKABLE SUCCESS.

Of all the lucky hunters I ever knew I accord the bun to Na-ta-way. He was one of the engaged servants at the post in Canada, and whenever he put on his snowshoes and sailed forth from the gates, some creature or bird would cross his path or vision. To do this and come within reasonable distance of Na-ta-way's small bore, muzzle-loading rifle was sure and speedy death to the unfortunate beast or bird.

I could never understand why he chose to be a servant in the Company in preference to being free to roam the lakes, rivers and forests, because had he elected to follow the occupation of a trapper and hunter he could not have failed to make double the money. Other Indians had traps set all around and quite near the post and yet Na-ta-way would kill as much as the average one, with only a poor half day off and his day on Sunday.

I never saw his equal for quickness in setting deadfalls or rabbit snares. However, this partakes more of a biography than what I set out to relate, and yet it is an indispensable digression to enable the reader to believe the wonderful and remarkable success this man had one day when he was given leave from daylight to night. There was a weighty reason for this extra freedom from duty for the fact was the post people were short of meat. The month was April and our frozen supply nearly used up.

Na-ta-way knew of a single moose yard, or more properly speaking, a yard with a single moose as occupant. To kill a lone moose on the crust does not require the combined efforts of two or more persons, therefore Na-ta-way was told to go and kill the moose and skin and quarter the animal, which considering the distance to go and come, amounted to a very good day's work. But Na-ta-way besides doing this and doing it well, accomplished much more.

Coming down from the moose mountain to get better walking, he crossed the fresh tracks of a large bear. This was nuts to our man. He immediately turned aside and followed up the trail, ramming down one of his little pea bullets as he went. The heat of the morning sun had softened the crust of the night and Mr. Bruin was making headway with difficulty. In fact, Na-ta-way had not gone over half a mile when he sighted the bear and was very soon close up to him.

The bear had two kind of ideas. One was to climb a tree and the second to run away, neither of which was carried into effect, for a bullet stopped the cowardly act of running, and a second one in the ear stilled him forever. The skin and the paws were all the hunter carried away. The meat would be got when the men came for the moose.

Na-ta-way was very soon swinging on down the mountain and struck a creek which emptied into one of a chain of lakes, that in turn drained into the big Ka-kee-bon-ga lake upon which the post was situated. Following down this creek he noticed ahead of him a mink, working his way up along the shore, noseing every hole as he came. Nothing was too big or too small for Na-ta-way. Poor little mink!

When he got abreast of the man on the ice, stood on its hind legs to get a better view of the strange object, but at that instant its sight became blurred, for it tumbled over dead. It was so full of life, energy and curiosity a few moments ago, was now being carried on the Indian's back, shoved into the folds of the bear skin.

But then, if we moralize, a man is walking with elastic step along a street when Presto! the heart stops, and he is being carried feet foremost by some three or four horror-struck pedestrians.

The hour was then high noon, snow soft and walking bad. Na-ta-way had covered several miles and done much since he had left his bed that morning. His inner man began to crave for food, the conditions were favorable, wood water and a sunny bank. What could be more alluring to a weary man? A bright fire was soon burning with the ever welcome tea kettle hanging in the blaze, the hunter on his knees in front waiting for it to boil.

Another digression right here. I never saw a man make tea, but after chucking in an ample quantity of the precious leaves from China, would throw in another pinch, either to make sure of there being a proper strength in the brew or for good luck. Be the reason what it may, they all do it. I do it myself.

Continuing on his march after his mid-day lunch, Na-ta-way came to a small lake. What is it that causes him to stop and cast his eyes about? The lake is full banks and therefore at that season must contain beaver. Yes, there stood the lodge on the opposite side and a well understood mark leading from the open water in front up into the bush. The beaver had come out the day before.

What Indian, or white man for that matter, can resist the chance offered to eat beaver meat? Na-ta-way looked at the Indians' clock, the sun, with a satisfied expression and his mind was made up; he would wait the coming ashore to feed. A comfortable spot was selected within gun shot of the place of debarkation. Here he tramped a hole in soft snow and strewed some balsam branches on the bottom upon which he crouched and waited.

There was no uncertainty as in the song the girl sang, "He cometh not," for he had hardly taken up his position before out struggled a young beaver and passed up the path leading to the young growth of trees. But Na-ta-way knew better than to fire at this one. No, the beaver passed on and up, giving grunts of anticipation. Number two came ashore and ambled inland without being molested. Now, however, Na-ta-way was all alertness. With his rifle cocked and his belt axe handy in front he waited the advent of another emblem of Canada. In a few minutes out he came to join his brothers or sisters who were already feasting on young sappy trees.

The crack of the rifle echoed far and near in the clear, mild atmosphere, but before it died away, the Indian stood over the shot beaver and barred the path against the frightened returning ones. The first coming down the hill he shot. The whole slaughter was well planned and carried out.

Three young beaver make a pretty solid lump on a man's back, but a hunter may leave moose meat and bear's meat in the bush to a chance wolf, but beaver, no! hardly! even if he has to make double trips. Na-ta-way had carried heavy weights slung by a portage strap across his forehead from childhood and could well support and carry what he now had.

I well remember that night when he entered our kitchen and let slide off his back that mixture of beaver, mink and bear skin. In fourteen hours he had walked about ten miles and killed: 1 moose, 1 mink, 1 bear and 3 beaver. Verily this was luck or success.

CHAPTER XVI.

THINGS TO AVOID.

WINTER.

Never leave your axe out doors all night. Intense cold makes it exceedingly brittle, most likely the first knot you put it into will cause a gash in the blade and an axe is an essential part of a trapper's outfit, and impossible to replace when far from settlements.

Never dry your snowshoes near the fire, but plant them some distance away to be dried by the frost. The fire acting on the dampness in the knitting cooks the fiber of the leather and causes the shoe to give out before its proper time.

Never, in very cold weather, carry your gun by the barrel; if occasion caused you to fire it off, the chances are the barrel will burst at the place where your hand heated the iron.

Never after wringing out your wet moccasins place them near the fire to dry, but scrape out any remaining moisture with the back of the sheathe knife, stuff each shoe with brush and hang at back of camp to dry gradually. The brush keeps the shoes extended and permits the heat to permeate to all parts.

Never put on the same shoe on the same foot two days in succession. The shoe will wear much longer and retain its shape by interchanging.

In wearing moose or deer skin shoes begin by wearing them wrong side out until almost worn through, then turn, and you have the grain side of the leather. Thus your shoe will last almost twice as long.

Never travel without an extra undershirt and a spare pair of socks; with the trunk and feet dry and warm there is some chance of salvation for a man if he was unfortunate enough to break through the ice or obliged to travel through the wet in the spring. The days may be mild enough but the nights are cold.

Never cut your night's wood from low ground bordering on water. It will cause you untold annoyance by continually shooting off live coals and sparks all over your blankets.

In selecting your camping place have your fire slightly higher than your bed. Most places, (unless on rock), are eaten away by action of the fire, and by the time you turn in you will have the fire on a level.

Never consider your work complete until you have an armful of fine cut up dry wood or a supply of birch bark handy. From excessive fatigue you may over-sleep and wake thoroughly chilled. In such an instance you want a quick bright fire, no fumbling about trying to ignite some half burnt sticks.

Never leave any excess of firewood lying on the snow to become sodden on the ground and covered by the following winter's snow, thus to be useless to you or anyone else passing that way. A few moments in the morning before taking the trail will stand it on end under some tree and it is good for future use.

Never underestimate your wood requirements for the night. It is better, yes, much better, to have a surplus than to turn out before daylight to replenish your fire.

Never, if you are dragging a toboggan or sleigh, leave it flat on its track where your day's march ends, but turn it on its side, if loaded, or stand it up, if empty, and scrape or rub off any frost on the bottom or runners. The next day it will slide easy, otherwise the empty sleigh alone will be a load.

Never put your game or fish to cook in boiling water. Place it, in preference, in cold and bring to the boil, then let it simmer till done.

I have seen the Indians on a very cold night, when on the trail, make a new fire where we had been sitting and spread our brush and blankets on the old fire place. The ground being thawed out our brush retained considerable warmth till morning.

Never, in the winter, make your camp fire directly under a large snow laden tree. The heat of the fire will melt the snow and the dropping water cause much annoyance and discomfort, or high winds may spring up before morning and send the snow about your fire and camp.

Never carry all your supply of matches about your person, have a few, even though only a half dozen, in some damp-proof article amongst your blankets. A very good receptacle if you have not a water proof box, is an empty Pain Killer vial. See that it is thoroughly dry, drop in your few matches and cork tightly.

This is for an emergency and can be carried about for months or years, and only opened under necessity, when perhaps one dry match will save your life.

Never leave your gun loaded in camp! The iron draws the dampness and im-parts it to the cartridges. Next day they may prove slow fire or not explode at all. Have your cartridges handy if you will, but really there is no necessity. The days of wolves and savage Indians are past and in most parts of the "wild" there is nothing to molest man.

One other axiom I will adduce and not prefix it with the negative "Never," because it is not always possible to adhere to this principle.

It is not generally known that the position one assumes when making one's bed has a great deal to do with getting a restful night's repose. When possible lie with your head to the north. The magnetic earth currents flow from the north, and thus from your head down through your body. The tired feeling you had when retiring has all flowed out through your feet before morning.

This fact may appear absurd to a person not giving the subject sufficient thought, but it is on the same principle as a person stroking your hair downwards. The result is quieting and soothing, but if he rubs it the contrary way it irritates and is hurtful.

I have proved the truth of this assertion many times during my nights on the trail. I have purposely rolled in my blanket with my head to the south, and arose the following morning, unrested, and my body "broken up."

The foregoing may be and is rather disjointed, because I have penned each subject as they came to my mind, but the reader may rest assured they are worth memorizing and were learned by the writer during long years of hardships.

SUMMER.

Suppose your canoe has been turned over on the beach all night, never launch it in the morning without first thoroughly examining the bottom from end to end. If there are rabbits or rats about, the place of a greasy hand is enough to draw them, and they will gnaw a lot of boat for very little grease.

This might be overlooked in the hurry of getting away, and the canoe either sink under you or sufficient water enter to damage your things.

Once my chum and I were making our way up river with our supplies. Amongst the provisions was a half barrel of pork. When camping the first night we left the pork near the overturned canoe. The rest of our outfit we carried up to our camp on the top of the river bank, thinking nothing would touch a solid hardwood barrel.

Well, in the grey morning, when we went to get water for our coffee we found the staves in shooks and the bricks of pork scattered about the gravelly beach. Rabbits had cut the hoops and the barrel had fallen to pieces. The rest was easy to the rabbit — not to us.

If you are a lone hunter never travel in summer without an extra paddle. You may lug this about all season and never require it but once, but that once you will be glad you have it.

Often when approaching game it is expedient to drop the paddle quietly in the water when taking up your gun. In the stillness of the wild, the noise of placing the paddle inboard is sufficient to scare away the game and the chance is lost. With a spare paddle at hand the hunter can quickly pursue the wounded game or paddle back and pick up the dropped paddle.

If you have a chum a second paddle is not necessary, as he can either forge the canoe ahead or back her to where you dropped yours.

Never talk or make unnecessary noise while hunting. Old hunters never do. It is only about the camp fire they talk, and even there always in a low tone of voice.

Old hunters communicate to one another all that is necessary by a shake of the canoe, a nod of the head or motions of the hands.

When portaging at a carrying place never when you get to the other end, put the canoe down at once, but let the man in front first scan carefully all about each side of the lake or river as far as the eye will carry. Something might be on the surface, standing in the shallows, or in the edge of the bush, which the noise of putting down the canoe would frighten away.

If you wish to avoid the dew of the morning, camp at the upper end of a carrying place, i. e., rapid, but if you wish to have a refreshing slumber camp at the foot of the rapid, have your head up stream and pointing to the north if possible.

Never push on and camp on the border of some small stagnant lake, merely to add a little length to your day's trail. Better camp this side and have living water for your cooking purposes.

If you were hunting in the fall in a beaver country and watching to shoot them in the evening:

Never, if it is a big lodge, fire at the first or even the second beaver that breaks water. If you do, good-bye to the others for that night. It is better to allow the first and second to swim away along shore to their wood-yards unmolested. The next to make its appearance will most likely be one of the old ones. This kill if you can, and then paddle slowly in the direction the first has taken. The chances are you will meet them coming back or see them ashore cutting wood.

See that your two or three traps are in good order, and leave the lake for your camp before darkness sets in.

Your camp should be half a mile away and to the leaward of the beaver lake.

In the spring of the year beaver begin to swim early in the afternoon and take to their lodge late in the morning. In the autumn when the nights are long they break water late and are not to be seen after sunrise next morning.

If you see two beaver at one time swimming and shoot one, leave it floating on the water. The chances are the second one will make a short dive, and you want to be ready with your gun when he comes up. I have often got one with each barrel this way.

By shooting in the evening and leaving three traps set I have cleaned out a lodge of seven beaver in an evening and a night, from 4 P. M. to 7 A. M. next morning, and this with only a boy of ten years old for a companion.

The hardest part was in packing them and my canoe out over five carrying places. But, oh! when the bunch was at the post what recompense, all those fine, rich furs and the luscious and sustaining meat, with a roasted tail now and again as a side bite.

Now penning these lines in my last camp in a town of ten thousand inhabitants, how my mind longs for one more season in the bush, but, alas! I fear it may never be.

CHAPTER XVII.

ANTICOSTA AND ITS FURS.

The island of Anticosta, lying in the mouth of the Gulf of St. Lawrence, runs parallel with the main land on its north shore and about twenty-five miles distant from it. Notwithstanding the close proximity to the continent and the straits, some winters blocked with ice fields, the martens on this island are peculiar and distinct in this manner, that almost without exception the forepaws and the end of the tail are tipped with white hair.

I traded one year several hundred pelts of Anticosta marten and with one or two exceptions they all showed this distinction from those we got on the north shore or mainland. I found this white ending of extremities even amongst the bears and foxes, and in some instances with the otter. Otherwise the marten are as well furred and as rich and deep in color as the far-famed Labrador ones.

Of bears there are on the island both black and brown; the latter are of immense size and very savage. One skin I got measured seven feet broad by nine feet long and showed the marks of no fewer than eleven bullet holes in his hide. The man from whom I purchased the skin told me he met the monster while traveling along the sea beach and fired at him. The bear dropped, but in a moment arose to his feet and rushed for the hunter. Fortunately there was a high rock near by, up which the man clambered with his gun, out of reach of the infuriated beast and from this "Coin de advantage" Arsenault loaded and fired round ounce balls into the bear until he was dispatched.

While on this trip I secured two of the finest and purest silver grey fox skins I ever handled. It is not generally known that a pure silver fox is much rarer than black or black silver. What I mean by pure silver is a fox that is silvered from the very head right down to the white tip of the tail. The majority of so-called silver foxes are black from the head to a third of the way down the back; a part of the body and rump alone being silvered.

In the Hudson's Bay Company trading posts, foxes are graded when purchased under the following names: black, black silver, silver grey, black cross, dark cross, ordinary cross, (first cousin to red) bright red, light red, white. I am aware that to make this list complete blue and grey foxes are wanting, but as they are only traded in one or two of the Company's posts and I was never at either, I will say nothing about them, but of the above grades and colors of foxes I have traded and trapped many.

A black cross is so very near a silver that it is only a savant that can tell the difference. A black cross has yellow hairs growing inside the ears and a patch of yellow near each fore leg, whereas a silver has none. Unscrupulous trappers very often try to get over these giving-away marks by plucking the hairs out of the ears and by greasing and smoking the side patches.

The first thing a trader does when a doubtful skin is offered is to look into the ears; if the hairs are wanting, he breathes on his hand and gently passes it down over the side. If the hand is blackened this is a proof number two and the smart "Alec" is found out.

Coming back to Anticosta; forty years ago the privilege of hunting was leased by the then owner of the seigniory to a man from Quebec, who each autumn repaired to the island with four or five men who hunted on shares, Mr. Corbett, supplying food, traps and ammunition, got a certain per cent. of the furs each caught.

They laid their small schooner up in a sheltered bay and Corbett used to cook and sweep the shanty while his men hunted and trapped.

Wrecks used to occur nearly every year of some late lumber-laden sailing vessel and in the spring, after the hunt was over, Corbett and his men would load their schooner with copper and iron from the hulls and sail for Quebec in June when the moderate summer winds had begun.

Five or six years ago M. Menier, the French chocolate king, purchased the island from the Seignorial heirs and has converted it into a game reserve. He has cut road, built wharfs and made many other improvements and is trying to acclimate animals that were not found on the island, such as moose, Virginia red deer, buffalo, beaver, etc.

A resident governor lives on the island the year around and has a steamer of a couple of hundred tons at his command that plies between the island and Quebec, as necessity requires. M. Menier, with a party of friends, comes from France each summer and passes a month on the island fishing and shooting. There are three salmon rivers, one where the fish are especially large and numerous.

After purchasing the island M. Menier secured from the Canadian Government the right to a three-mile belt of water, so when the owner is on "Anticosta" he is actually lord and master of all that he surveys.

*　　　*　　　*　　　*　　　*

In the *Forest and Stream* of Feb. 9 I have read the article written by H. de Puyjalon on the pekan or fisher. Mr. de Puyjalon appears to me to have attempted writing upon a subject in which he was very little versed and with no data upon which to base his assertions. As a matter of fact, prior to about the year 1860, the fisher or pekan was an animal unknown to the trappers on the north shore and Labrador, east of the Saguenay, and it was only after that year that an odd one was trapped in that lower country. In fact, when first the fisher made its appearance the Indians had no name for it, but after it became better known they adopted the Algonquin name it now bears. When an Indian, in the early sixties, was fortunate enough to have one in his pack he mentioned it as a big marten.

For many years the Saguenay River appeared to have been the boundary line for moose, red deer and pekan, none being known on the east side, while fairly numerous on the west bank. As the fisher was never very plentiful on the Labrador, and when found was only in the wooded part, it is not strange that a person of Mr. de Puyjalon's sedentary habits should have trapped only two.

I lived within hearing distance (that is, courier's reports) of Mr. de Puyjalon, while that gentleman resided on the coast, and apart from hearing that he set a fox trap or two about his shanty, never heard him mentioned as what we would call a trapper.

In his article he gives the pekan the credit of showing considerable cunning and finesses. As a matter of natural history they have no more of this than a marten, and will bungle into an ordinarily made dead-fall in the same way. The only thing to do when fisher are known to be about a line of marten traps is to make a larger sized house for him and extra heavy weight to keep him down when caught.

That the fisher decreases in number is quite contrary to facts. According to the last London sales of mixed furs in September, fisher stood at 4,926, in 1893 4,828, and in 1883 4,640, showing that they have increased slightly. In some parts of the country they stand in the returns about equal to the marten exported. I remember this very plainly, for at the time it struck me as peculiar. I was in charge of an outpost on Lake Superior. Our returns were principally beaver, foxes and lynx, very few marten, and in that year I had at the close of trade 96 marten and 96 fisher. This was impressed on my memory as being a strange coincidence, because the post I had been previously stationed at turned out over two thousand marten to eight or ten fisher. The prices for fisher in the Canadian market vary but little and we never have fluctuations as in silver foxes and marten. The skins are little used in any country except Russia and China, where they are used chiefly by the rich as coat linings. As they have a tough skin, and when prime a deep, rich fur, it is a wonder — since they are comparatively few on the market — that they do not command a better price.

The resort of the pekan is principally along the mountain ranges, never in the black spruce or flat barren country of the table land or to the north of it. Their food consists of rabbits, partridges, mice, squirrels and fruit when in season. When the mountain ash berries are plentiful and hang late in the autumn, both the fisher and the marten are difficult, if not impossible, to trap, as there is no meat lure you can bait with, that will induce them to leave the berries.

In a year of scarcity of fruits, when the fisher has to depend on his own adroitness in securing his food, I have read the signs and seen where one has been very persistent in running down a rabbit, the chase being up and down, in and out, until bunny was overtaken, killed and eaten.

CHAPTER XVIII.

CHISELLING AND SHOOTING BEAVER.

It is only in the far back country that the once plentiful beaver are to be found at the present day, and though a description of one of the modes the Indians adopt in killing them may be of no practical use to the present generation of hunters on the fringe of civilization, it will at least be interesting to them and remembered by some old-timers. Chiselling, or trenching, beaver, as it is sometimes called, is yet followed by the interior Indians, and when conditions are favorable, is a most expeditious way of piling up a whole lodge.

The writer in his young days has many a time accompanied the Indians on these hunts, and the description of my last participation in this exciting mode of hunting I will endeavor to explain to the reader. I found a large lodge of beaver in a very small lake, probably a quarter of a mile long by one-eighth wide. It was so late in the fall that it was too near freezing to set traps in open water, and the appearance of the shore conveyed to my experienced eye that it could be chiselled to advantage. I therefore returned to the post and left the beaver undisturbed.

It was fortunate I did so, for the following night all the small ponds and lakes in the vicinity were ice-bound only to open again in six months. A few days after an Indian visited the post for an additional supply of ammunition and snaring twine, and I took the opportunity to enlist his services to kill my beaver. I offered him two pounds of tea for a day's work at the lake. Whether he killed the beaver or not, he was sure of the tea. This he agreed to, and I immediately put together the necessary things so as to make an early start.

As the lake was only an hour's walk from the post we reached it about sunrise, and both knowing our business, set to work at once. The implements necessary for each man are a belt axe, an ordinary socket mortise chisel one and a quarter inch broad. This is handled (generally at the lake) with a peeled spruce sapling from six to seven feet long, and last but by no means least, is a good beaver dog, and almost any Indian dog is good for beaver, as they learn from the older ones and train themselves. I had two at the post and these, of course, accompanied us. The first thing to do is to visit the discharge of the lake. If this is dammed a trap must be set at the opening where the water escapes. This is the first precaution, so that if any beaver during the trenching process tries to escape down the creek he must pass over the trap and get caught.

Where the water of the lake and that of the creek is of the same level there is consequently no dam, and then the creek, at its narrowest part, has to be picketed from side to side. This is often a laborious job, as pickets have to be cut and carried to the creek, a cut three or four inches wide made in the ice and then the pickets driven down side by side, or very close to each other, so the beaver cannot possibly pass.

This work done to our satisfaction, our next point was the lodge itself. This we broke in from the top and all the sticks, mud, etc., we jammed down in the opening or exit. This is done to prevent the beaver returning once they have left the lodge. At several places around the lake the beavers have what the Indian call "washes." These are burrows they make beneath the surface, generally up under the roots of a large tree. They use them for breathing places and to retire to if disturbed at the lodge. They make these at any favorable spot where the conditions are suitable, and the "washes" vary in number from three to five up to twice that number.

The dog's share of the work is to travel around the lake and scent the beaver under the frozen bank. He is trained not to give tongue, he merely points and sets his head on one side, then the other. Both our dogs are now pointing and we hastened over to the spot. A hole is chisselled in the ice close to shore and a crooked stick inserted. This stick is cut at the commencement of the hunt, is about seven feet long, and has a natural curve, almost as much as a half moon. The end of the stick is moved about, it slips up under the bank; this is the entrance to the "wash." We cut the hole in the ice larger and then watch the water. If the beavers (or even one) are up in the bank there is a perceptible rise and fall of the water at the opening. We then set to work to fence in the entrance to the "wash" with sticks. This done, the ice is cut away inside the stakes, a couple of feet square.

All is now ready for the test. The Indian bares his arm up to the arm pit. He gets down on his knees over the hole and watches, while I go up a few feet from the bank and drive the chisel into the ground. This disturbs the beaver and he makes a mad drive to get out to the lake. The pickets bring him up, and while he is turning about, puzzled and bewildered, the Indian dashes his arm into the water and seizing the beaver by the hind leg gives one strong pull and lands him over his head. The fall on the ice stuns him momentarily, and before he can escape the Indian has dealt him a blow with the head of his axe. The young ones are generally the first killed, as two or three may be together in one "wash." The old ones, as a rule, give much trouble, as they vacate one "wash" for another at the approach of the hunter. Then there is nothing for it but to picket off each "wash" as found, and thus reduce the number of places for him to resort to.

A hunter with a practiced eye can tell pretty well by the appearance of the shores about a beaver lake if the "washes" are few in number or numerous and guides himself accordingly. If the lake has drained a foot or two since the ice took, it is useless to attempt to chisel, as the beaver can go ashore under the ice anywhere and breathe. In our case all circumstances were favorable; the water was full under the ice, all over, and the "washes" were very few and easily located.

By three o'clock in the afternoon we had the beavers all killed, two old and four young ones. We really had five by dinner time, so we lit a fire, boiled our kettle and let the last old one quiet down a bit while we ate our lunch. We got him at last in the last "wash," and I suppose knowing this was his last stand he would not attempt to leave the back part of the hole no matter how much I poked the chisel in about him. So while the Indian kept a close and alert watch at the mouth of the "wash," I made a large opening at the back and slipped in one of the dogs. In a moment beaver and dog were both out at the entrance fighting in the water. The beaver fastened his terrible teeth in the dog's lip. The Indian and I each managed to grasp a hind leg, a long pull and out came beaver and dog together. We had to force his teeth apart after killing him before the dog was free.

*　　　*　　　*　　　*　　　*

I mentioned in a previous article that I would at some future time tell of the part a beaver-dam enacts in the successful shooting of the beaver.

As I said, the beaver has to keep a jealous watch on the dam to preserve the proper height of the water at their lodge. They make nightly visits to see all is well, just as a faithful watchman goes his rounds of the factory over which he has charge.

Any sudden falling of water brings the beaver down post haste to the dam to repair the damage or leak. Often an otter is the cause of the trouble, as they sometimes bore a passage way under the discharge, thereby letting out a large quantity of water in a very short while.

The Indians, knowing this careful watchfulness of the beaver, use it to his destruction by purposely breaking a portion of the dam and hiding, await the coming of the little builders, shooting them at close range.

I cannot do better than to describe one of these shootings, in which I took part.

One of the principal things to observe is that the wind should be in the proper direction, i. e., from the lodge toward the dam. A day coming when the condition of the wind was favorable, we set off with our double-barrel guns, a tea kettle and some grub, and reached the discharge about 3 P. M.

The little pond was brimming full with the proper quantity of water, flowing out of the cut to insure a regular equality. The Indian studied all this, looked at the sun, and decided it was yet too early to cut the dam, and in the meantime we fixed a nice brush cache at different angles to the dam, wherein we were to sit and watch. About four o'clock the Indian hacked away at the discharge with a small pointed stick, prying several holes under and about it, and in a short time the creek below the dam became a highly turbulent stream, and then we retired to our bedded places and waited.

I might mention that the time of the year was about the tenth of October, a time when beaver are quite prime, in that north country.

We had to wait possibly an hour before the first beaver made his appearance. It was one of the parents, and judging by the speed at which he came down the pond, he must have been of turbine construction. One thing sure he was on a rush message, and wanted to get there quick. I saw the Indian's gun barrel move slightly, and when the beaver got within close distance he pulled on him, and in a few minutes the beaver lay awash close to the dam, where he was allowed to remain.

The next one that came in sight was a young one, and came my way. He met the same fate. The slight current dragged him also close to the dam, a few feet from his father or mother, as the case might be.

This double bagging was hardly over when another big one came around a point heading for the dam as the others had done. This fellow proved to be my meat also, and again a pause in the shooting.

The shadows of the evening were fast falling and we had almost given up hopes of seeing any others, when again we saw a far-off ripple of some animal swimming, and it proved to be another young one. This one took down the shore nearest to the Indian, and beat the water at his gun's shot.

The sport was becoming quite exciting, and I would have had no objection to continuing it longer, but the Indian arose and called across to me to gather up our beaver, having a large and a small one each, a very fair division.

He then set to work to repair the damaged dam as well as he could, and explained to me that the remaining ones would finish off the job when the fear was off of them.

The Indian said that amongst his tribe the hunters often used this mode of hunting, and what beaver was left unkilled they either trapped later on or trenched them out when the ice set fast. One thing I learned from that afternoon's hunt was that it was simple and successful, and I used the knowledge several times, in other years, to my advantage.

We had to pack those beaver through four miles of trackless bush, and each pack must have weighed ninety pound, and, as far as I remember, we rested only three times. I mention this because I saw in one of the letters that appeared in H-T-T, where a man mentions having killed a beaver that weighed fifty pounds, which was so heavy he had to drag it home.

I have heard of dragging a deer or hair seal, but never of a fur-bearing animal. I wonder what that man would have thought to see an Indian of a hundred and thirty-six pounds weight carry four beaver and his bark canoe on top, over a three-quarter mile portage without resting, and he did not even appear winded at the end. The beaver weighed in the neighborhood of one hundred and eighty pounds, and the bark canoe an easy sixty, but then they are inured to carrying heavy loads from childhood.

CHAPTER XIX.

THE INDIAN DEVIL.

My companion and I were sitting late one afternoon at a beaver lake, waiting for the sun to get near the tree tops before pushing our canoe into the lake to watch for beaver. They generally break water near the lodge about sundown and swim along shore to cut their food, and one has usually a chance of a shot.

All at once we heard back in the bush a cracking and breaking of branches, readily understood as done by a large animal running through the underbrush at a high rate of speed. The noises came nearer and nearer, a little off to our right, and I grasped my double-barreled gun which lay beside me and waited events.

A few moments after we saw a large caribou break cover about one hundred yards to the right and spring into the lake. But what was that black object clinging to his neck? Surely some animal!

The caribou struck out as fast as it could swim, heading for the further shore, and we jumped into our canoe and gave pursuit. The keen eyes of the animal on the caribou's neck having detected us, it relinquished its hold, dropped off into the water and turned for the shore the caribou had left.

The canoe was immediately headed to cut off his retreat, and when within proper distance I shot it with one barrel and left it there dead on the surface of the lake, while we continued on our chase.

This diversion had taken our attention from the caribou, but now, when we had resumed the chase, we found the animal was getting through the water very slowly, and as we were paddling in its wake, we perceived the water at each side of the canoe was bloody. By the time we reached the caribou it was dead.

On examination we found the jugular vein had been cut by the fierce animal on its back, and it had bled to death, fleeing with what strength it had to the last drop of the poor thing's blood.

We threw a string over its horns and towed it back to the portage, picking up in passing our floating black animal, which proved to be a very large wolverine, carcajo or Indian devil, the beast going under all of these names with hunters and traders.

The carcajo, when he loads for deer, goes down to one of their runways, or on a road leading to a salt lick. He climbs a tree and gets out on some branch over-hanging the track. Here he flattens himself out and waits. Yes, he is a record waiter. He can give points to even the girl who is waiting and watching.

Time is no object to him; his inwards may be shriveling up for want of food, but there he remains. Once he has taken up that position nothing but a deer will make him show the least sign of life. He is to all intents a part of the tree limb, and the knowledge that all things "come to him who waits" is strongly fixed in his devil brain.

The deer passes, he drops on to him like a rock. Should he strike too far back, his cruel claws grip his way up toward the neck, and there he settles himself, a fixture, and cuts away at the large veins till the poor deer bleeds to death.

As soon as the deer feels this foreign weight on his back the cruel teeth cutting into him, he at once runs into and through the thickest part of the forest trying to rub the incubus off his back. But the carcajo has the tenacity of the bulldog, and his own skin would be ripped and lacerated before he would let go his hold.

The deer, realizing this mad rush through the bush is useless, makes for the nearest water in the hope that this will rid him of his enemy. But vain hope, the wolverine is there to stop, and only opens his jaws when the deer is dead, or, as in my instance, through fear for his personal safety.

Our beaver hunt was spoilt for that night, so we moved back on the trail and camped. There we passed our time drying the deer's meat and skinning the Indian devil.

*   *   *   *   *

The amount of destructiveness contained in a full grown wolverine, or, as he is sometimes called, carcajo and Indian devil, is something past belief to any one who has not lived in the country in which they resort. The tales told by hunters and lumbermen of the doings of this strong and able beast would fill pages. Some of these, like fish stories, may be seasoned by a pinch of salt, therefore I will only jot down a few that I experienced personally in my trapping days.

Hunger cannot always be adduced as a reason for their thieving propensities, inasmuch as they will steal martens, rabbits and partridges out of traps and snares when they are full to repletion just out of pure cussedness, as it were, to make the owner of the traps and snares to use unseeming language.

When once a wolverine gets on a line of deadfalls the trapper has either to abandon his traps and seek new fields, or kill the mischievous animal, for even should the line be ten miles long the Indian Devil will destroy or put out of order each trap to the very end. Their favorite plan is to tear out the back of the trap. If they find a marten caught and they are not hungry, they will carry it off at right angles to the trail and bury it in the snow, or climb a tree and deposit it on a cross branch. I have found no fewer than three martens when visiting my trap road a day after the wolverine had passed.

Once when chum and I were off for a couple of nights from our main camp, on our return we missed a toboggan from in front of the shanty door. This was passing strange as no Indians were in the vicinity, nor had passed our way. Hunt as we did in every conceivable place did not produce the missing sled. It was only two years after when camping in the same place and felling a dry spruce for firewood that the toboggan and tree came to earth together. The mystery was solved, a wolverine had drawn it up in the top branches of the tree and left it.

I remember a laughable occurrence that took place once. Chum and I had a small log shanty on the edge of a big lake. This was our headquarters. Radiating from the shanty we had lines of traps to the four points of the compass and we often slept out a night, visiting and cleaning out the traps. Each used to take a line end, each slept for that night solitary in the wilds.

On our return from one of our trips we met on the edge of the clearing and when we got to our shanty we noticed things looked strange and yet we could not tell for a moment what it was. On opening the door things looked stranger still, for on the floor was a mixture of mostly all our belongings, flour, matches, moccasins, tobacco, soap and numerous other things and sifted over all was ashes.

One would think a hurricane had come down the chimney and blown everything loose, but we knew better. Some animal must have done this devastation and we could call that animal by his right name by reading his work. Yes, a wolverine had been there and we fell to calling him some appropriate names and as we went along, we invented other names which our cuss vocabulary did not possess.

During a momentary lull in our burst of passion, we heard a slight scratching under the table and there we found the worker of all the mischief. A blow of the axe finished him then and there and he was pulled out into the light. Our surprise was great to find most of the hair on his head singed off and he was blind in both eyes. Then we set to work to read the signs how it happened.

We found by our deduction that in the first place he had clambored up on to the roof and from there had entered by the wide mouthed chimney. Once in the shanty he had set to work to examine and investigate everything about, each in turn to be cast from him on the floor.

The very last thing to attract his attention was my chum's powder horn. It was one of those old-fashioned cow horns with a plug in the small end. There was at the time nearly half a pound of gun powder in it. With this bright and shining article "carajou" started to clambor up and out thru the chimney.

Alas! he held the butt end upwards. By dryness, I suppose, the plug dropped out and a fine stream of powder found its way to the center of our fireplace where a few coals must have yet kept fire. A flame shot up, an explosion followed, and down came the frightened, blinded beast. No doubt from agony and fear he crawled under the table where we found him and put an end to his misery.

Their legs are very strong and muscular and I have known them to break out of even a No. 4 Newhouse. When they will take bait a pretty sure way to get them is by "setting a gun," but this is dangerous work as some stranger might pass that way, and even to the person setting the gun, great care must be used.

As they are very seldom famished and therefore will not take bait, about the only thing for the trapper to do is to give him the "right of way," and the hunter to move to some other part of the country for a month or so. We call them the Indian Devil because he inhabits the Indian country, but the Indians themselves call them

"Bad Dog," this being the lowest and meanest name their language supplies.

CHAPTER XX.

A TAME SEAL.

Many years ago, before the great River Moisie was resorted to by cod fisher-men and others, the harbor seals used to come up the stream in great numbers for the purpose of bringing forth their young in its quiet upper pools. After staying with their young for a couple of weeks, the mother seals would return down the river, and a few days later the little baby seals would drift down with the current and be carried out to sea, there to hunt and grow big, and in their turn become father and mother seals and visit their native river.

Many a calm evening I have stood on the gallery outside the house and listened to the infant-like cry of the poor little seals as they drifted on the river past the post. One evening, toward the end of "the run" we heard one crying in a most pitiful and heart-rending way. Every now and then we could see the snow-white mite as he floated on the surface near mid-stream.

I got a large salmon scoop and joined the man on the beach. We waited till the seal had floated past us, then quietly pushed out the boat. The man headed obliquely down stream to come up with the baby from behind, while I took a position in the bow, ready to land it in the boat. In a few minutes we were up to him. The poor little deserted fellow was pawing about in the water much after the manner of a blind puppy and uttering plaintiff cries, startlingly like a real baby. I skipped the scoop well under him, and in a moment he was safely landed in the bottom of the boat.

I fixed up an extemporary feeding bottle, made of a piece of rubber tubing, a cork and an empty soda water bottle, which we filled with some nice warm milk. We got him comfortable on a sheepskin alongside the kitchen stove, and with a little instruction he very soon knew how to work his end of the tube. The warmth of the stove and the bottle of milk very quickly sent him into sweet forgetfulness.

My first intention was to keep him only a few days, until he got a little larger and stronger, and then let him continue his journey to the sea. But the little fellow became such a pet and evidently liked his surroundings so well that it would have been heartless in the extreme to send him away; so Jack, as the cook christened him, became one of the family, and grew and waxed strong, and followed me about between the buildings with his flopping gait in a most ridiculous manner.

In September, numbers of fine sea trout used to come in the river each tide and go out with the ebb. We placed a stand of old useless salmon nets near the last sand point to create a back-water, from which to fly-fish. Jack used to accompany me on these fishing tours, and he very soon came to understand what my whipping the water was for.

One day he wabbled down to the very edge of the river, gazed up and down and across the water, and the next instant dived in, with a greasy, sliding motion. The waters closed over him, and I paused in my pastime to see what would happen next. I looked about in all directions for Jack, but not a ripple disturbed the placid waters. He could not have been meshed in the folds of the net, because I would have seen the floats vibrate. So I stood there pondering, my thoughts partly perplexed and partly sorrowful for the possible loss of our pet.

All at once I heard heavy breathing almost at my feet, and looking down, there was Jack with a fine 3½ lb. sea trout crossways in his mouth, which, on my calling his name, he deposited at my feet. Then you may be sure I petted the dear young fellow, and he seemed to understand that what he had done was appreciated by his master, for after rolling himself for a few moments on the sand he made another dive, and another, and another, always with the same successful results, and the best part of his fishing was that he only selected the largest and fattest fish. We went home, both very proud in our own way — Jack for having been made so much of, and I because of the useful accomplishment of my pet.

As long as the run of fish continued, Jack and I used to resort each day to the eddy. He brought the fish ashore and I put them in the basket. What we could not consume at the house, the cook salted for winter use. Yes, the winter was coming on, and the thought occurred to me several times what we would do with Jack. Jack, however, made no attempt to take his freedom and forsake us. On the contrary, he manifested greater affection for us all, and, as the days became shorter and the nights colder and longer in that northern latitude, he used to sleep for many hours on a stretch, huddled up with the dogs in the kitchen, only going out of doors for an occasional slide in the snow once or twice during the course of each day.

Even the long winter of the North comes to an end in time, and once again we had open water; the last-bound river was again free from ice, and Jack used to take long swims, but he always came back. Finally the run of salmon struck the river, and I took Jack down to the bight of the sandbars to fly him at bigger game than the trout. He made one or two dives and came ashore empty-mouthed. He saw there were no caresses for Jack, so he tried again.

This time his efforts were crowned with success, for he landed with a 12 lb. salmon struggling in his strong jaws. He received my pating and expressions of satisfaction with unbounded joy and seemed to know he had done something to be proud of, for he ambled up the sandbank and slid down to the water several times in rapid succession.

Soon it was the season for the seals to enter the river as in past years, and the Indians were shooting them from their canoes whenever they had a chance. Jack used to go so far afield now, probably trying to find the mother that had so shamefully deserted him last year, that we feared he might be shot by the Indians by mistake; so we tied a piece of blue worsted gartering about his neck to distinguish him from the other seals. But alas for the poor Knight of the Garter. One day Jack was out among the other seals off the mouth of the river, and in some way the blue garter must have been detached from his neck, for an Indian shot him.

The man brought him ashore and told us of the mishap. As soon as he handled him to put him in the canoe, he knew at once from the roughness of his coat it was poor Jack. And thus ended our intelligent and useful pet.

We buried him near the flagstaff and put up a board bearing the inscription "Jack."

*   *   *   *   *

Seeing a small shark brought ashore the other day by one of the salmon fishermen, who had found it rolled up in his net, put me in mind of an exciting adventure I had many years ago. Both at the east, as well as the west side of the mouth of the great River Moisie, sand banks run out to sea for a distance of two or three miles. These are covered at high tide, but being of almost a uniform height, the falling tide runs off of them in a very short space of time, and leaves them dry with the exception of some odd places where pools of water remain. The banks are dry the last two hours of the ebb and the first two hours of the flood tide.

The great river continually deposits on these sands such quantities of vegetable matter, that they are a resort for many kinds of small fishes; and numerous waterfowl come there at certain stages of the tide to feed on the fish.

I was only about eighteen at the time, and had gone out in a birch-bark canoe to shoot ducks on the banks. My companion, an Indian boy, even younger than myself in years, but several times older in experience, was to steer the canoe. The last words his father said to us before leaving, were, "Don't go too far out, or the 'Ma-thcie-ne-mak' will cut your canoe and eat you."

The sea that morning was as calm as a pond, and perfectly glassy from the strong May sun striking straight down on it. We had been out for a couple of hours, and had had pretty fair luck with sea-ducks and loons, and were just about starting for the shore before the tide left us dry on the banks. If such a thing had happened, it would have entailed on us the labor of carrying our canoe a mile or so to the beach, over soft yielding sand.

"We better go," the boy was saying when his words were cut short in his mouth. With the remains of that breath he screeched "Ma-tchie-ne-mak!" and started to paddle like one possessed. I admit that his fright was infectious, and coupled with the dread name of shark, it so quickened my stroke, that Hanlon's sixty-a-minute were very slow compared to the way I worked my paddle. I have read, and heard from old whalesmen, that as long as one kept the water churned up, there was no danger of the shark getting in his work. Twice the boy called out, "There he is!" Once I caught a glimpse of the monster a few yards off on our port beam, heading to the shore also, but evidently watching for a chance to attack us.

The tide was now running out, and consequently the more we neared the shore, the shoaler the water got. The shark had not stopped to consider this in his mad rush to catch us. At last our canoe grounded on the sands and we looked back with relief at our narrow escape. But, ah! what is that about a couple of acres astern, surely not the shark! But it was, and he was floundering about in shallow water, in one of the pools, and every minute the water was getting less. "Hoop-la! we will now hunt the shark," I said to little Moses, as I started off toward him over the now dry sands.

Yes, there he was, the great, ugly beast, flopping about in a basin surrounded by banks, out of which it was impossible for him to escape. From the shore the boy's father and one of my men saw what was going on and came out with a handful of bullets and their guns. In the meantime I was employing the time with good results, by pouring into the shark charge after charge of AAA shot at close range.

By the time the men reached us the fish was pretty sick, and apart from snapping his immense jaws, was lying perfectly still. The first bullet from a distance of ten feet put an end to him. When the tide came in again we towed him into the river and cut him up and salted the chunks in barrels to feed the dogs the next winter. From the liver we rendered out three gallons of oil as clear as water. This of itself was of value to us the next winter in our lamps, it gave a clear light and emitted no smoke. Those were the days before coal oil came into general use. Our only lights at the post were home-made tallow candles, or a cotton rag from a tin spout fed by seal-oil. This, combined with the burning rag, gave off a heavy, dense, black smoke, which was, if not injurious, very unpleasant to inhale during the long winter evenings. The shark-oil being so much superior, I kept it for my own private lamps, and the teeth ornamented the mantlepiece.

CHAPTER XXI.

THE CARE OF BLISTERED FEET.

Much suffering and discomfort are experienced by the novice on snowshoe tramps by the want of knowledge as to how to care for and protect the feet from blistering.

The toes are the parts that suffer most from the friction of the cross snowshoe strings that are continually see-sawing the front part of the moccasin, and many, from an erroneous idea of cause and effect, pile on extra socks, thinking thereby to prevent the blistering by the thickness of their foot padding.

During my first years in the Hudson Bay service I suffered like any other new "hitter" of the long trail, but once started on the tramp there was no giving in. Places being hundreds of miles apart, there were no houses nor any place to stop and say, "I can go no further." On a journey of seven, eight or ten days, we took probably one day's extra provisions, but no more, therefore be the back lame through the heavy bundle it had to support day after day, or our every toe blistered to the bone, walk on we must and did. I have often seen the blood appear on my moccasins, working its way through three or four pairs of socks and become so dried and caked that before the shoes could be removed at the night's camp-fire, warm water had to be poured freely upon the moccasin to release the foot.

The agony at such times was past explaining. It was quite a work to patch up each separate toe with balsam gum and rag before turning in for the night, and yet stiff, swollen and sore, these poor feet had to have the large heavy snowshoes suspended to them next morning and the weary tramp continued as on the previous day.

Our guides, the Indians, did not suffer, as their feet were hardened from childhood, and as an Indian never gives advice nor offers to relieve his companion's load without being asked, we, the unfortunate greenhorns, were compelled to trudge on in the wake of our pace-maker as well as we could.

Of course I tried by all manner of changes in footwear to alleviate the trouble by taking off some thickness of socks and by putting on extra ones, all to no avail. Trip after trip, and year after year, I suffered with cut toes and blistered feet. By good fortune, I think it was my fifth year in the country, I was ordered from St. Lawrence posts to meet a winter packet party from Hudson's Bay. A certain lake on the divide was arranged for in the autumn as the meeting place of the two parties. The packeters from Hudson's Bay were to leave on the 3d of January and had a journey ahead of them of 325 miles. My party, two Indians and self, left on the 6th of January, having 55 miles less to travel, or 270 miles. Our day's tramps were so similar in length that we arrived at the rendezvous within four hours of each other.

One of the party from the bay was a Scotch half-breed, and from him, for the first time, I learned the art of caring properly for the feet. He made me cast aside all my woolen knitted socks, and out of his abundance he supplied me with smoked fawn-skin socks, ankle high, made in the fashion of a moccasin, only with no tops or welts of seams. The top and bottom pieces of leather were herring-boned together, a slit was made in the top half to insert the foot and this was put on the bare foot. On top of this two other shoe socks, made of duffle or blanketing, were placed and the moose skin moccasin over all, the leather top of which was tied about the naked ankle.

I ventured to opine that I would possibly be cold there, or freeze, but my new friend told me the object was to keep the feet from over heating. "And this and the knitted socks is the cause of all your suffering."

"Now listen to me," he went on; "at every noon day fire, or in fact any time a lengthened halt is called, sit on the brush before the fire and take off both moccasins and all your socks, turn them inside out and beat them on a stick or the brush to take out all the creases the feet have made. Let them cool wrong side out and while this is taking place, have your feet also cooling. Let them become thoroughly cold before replacing your socks and shoes and when doing this put those that were on the right foot on to the left, and vice versa. This affords a wonderful relief to the tired feet and you resume the journey with a rested feeling. At night, after the last pipe is smoked and you are about turning in to get what sleep you can with no roof to cover you but the far-off heavens, then turn up your pants to the knee and jump, bare-footed and bare-legged into the nearby snow and stand in it until you can bear it no longer, then stand near the blazing camp-fire and with a coarse towel, or bag, rub the legs and feet well until the blood is tingling, and the color of your lower extremities resembles a boiled lobster, and my word for it, you will rest better, sleep sounder and arise refreshed — what you never enjoyed before."

Fitted out as I was and following his advice of the snow bath, I made the return journey with ease and pleasure. I made long tramps for twenty years following and never again was I troubled by either blisters or cut feet. Even making short trips about the post hunting, I never allowed a knitted sock near my feet.

CHAPTER XXII.

DEER-SICKNESS.

The Indian term "deer-sickness" is in reality a misnomer, as it is not the deer that is sick but the party following its tracks. The idea of writing this article came to me by reading "Scent Glands of the Deer," which appeared in *Forest and Stream* of May 13, and I remembered how I had the deer-sickness thirty-eight years ago.

There are many surprises for a tenderfoot or greenhorn in the wild, but the name given to one of these very-much-to-be-pitied parties in the bush country from the Labrador to Lake Superior is *mangers du lard*. This is the universal cognomen by which a stranger in the north country is known. I found by tracing back that this soubriquet was first given by the French *courriers du bois* to a new hand entering the back country for the first time.

It is said that in those early days the French youths, from which new hands were recruited, lived at home on very scanty food, and when they got away working for the fur company, where pork was, comparatively, in abundance, they let their young appetites loose and ate the flesh of swine in prodigious quantities, whereby they became known as *mangers da lard*, i. e., pork eaters, and this denoted a stranger or greenhorn, the tenderfoot of the Western prairie.

I was somewhat of a greenhorn myself and suffered thereby by catching the deer-sickness. Like a good many other bad knocks that a beginner has to endure, this bit of sickness had an abiding effect on me and was never repeated.

My experience came about in this wise. I had accompanied a family of Indians to a deer battue, and after the general slaughter was over I was allotted the duty of following up a wounded deer; by the word deer I mean a wood caribou.

This particular buck had been shot at close quarters, the ball going clear through its stomach. While the shot had the effect of bowling the deer over it had not touched a vital spot, and during the excitement of the other shooting the animal got up and traveled away unobserved. The snow was pretty deep, nevertheless the further the deer went the better he appeared to get along. When this fact became evident to me, who was following his track, literally with my nose to the snow, I put on a greater spurt to try and end the jig. The deer by this time had become cognizant of being followed and he also increased his pace.

I now became aware of a weakness in my limbs, a nauseating smell in my nostrils and a faint and giddy sensation in my head. This uncomfortable feeling grew worse, and at last to save myself from falling I had to lean against a tree and wipe my brow with a handful of snow.

This had a momentary good effect. I saw clearly once more and pushing ahead redoubled my efforts to come within shooting distance of my deer. But I had not gone far before I felt a relapse coming and in a few moments I was in worse distress than ever. The last I remember was seeing a whirl of trees going around me. It was the last conscious moment before I fainted dead away and fell in my tracks in the snow.

Luckily the chief had sent his two boys to follow me up, not that he anticipated this ending, but for the purpose of skinning and cutting up the deer. It was providential he did, for otherwise I would never have awakened in this world. As it was, the cold had thoroughly penetrated my body and it was only after drinking a quart or two of hot tea that circulation resumed its functions.

After I had come around to the youth's satisfaction the eldest one started off after the cause of all my trouble, leaving his younger brother to replenish the fire and attend to my wants. The elder boy returned after an hour or two, having killed the deer, the proof, the split heart tucked in his belt. Darkness was then setting in, but the boys made ready to start for camp. What had taken me hours of toil to cover, they passed over in a very short time; in fact, we only saw my trail once or twice on the way out to the lake.

That night, after supper the chief told me of the "deer-sickness," and warned me against persistently following the trail. He continued and told how the Indians did and in after years I saw their mode and practiced it myself. He explained to be that a pungent odor exuded from the deer's hoofs when they were pursued and it was this that caused my weakness and distress.

The Indians in following deer cut the trail once in a while merely to make sure they are going in the right direction and to ascertain the freshness of the tracks. This is done with a two-fold purpose, first to avoid the odor from the fresh tracks and secondly to run or walk in the most open parts of the forest. Moose, caribou, and deer when fleeing from an enemy invariably pass through the thickest bush, because the snow is shallower under thick, branchy trees than in the open, therefore the Indian walks a spell on the right hand side of the trail, then crosses over and passes on the left.

From the topography of the country the Indian has a pretty good idea of the trend of the caribou's course, and the cutting of the trail from time to time is only to assure himself that he is correct in his surmise, and to judge by the tracks how near he is to the quarry. He thereby passes through the clearest country, has the best walking and escapes the nauseous effluvia emitted from the animals' hoofs.

*   *   *   *   *

It falls to us who live in the country the year round to hear amusing stories from the guides of their experiences with the "tenderfeet" that visit the north country during the open season. One that showed the cuteness of the guide was told me shortly ago by the man himself.

Dr. S---- came to Roberval with the expressed wish of taking home a caribou head of his own killing. He engaged George Skene as man of all work, and Old Bazil, the noted guide and successful hunter.

Although it is not customary for guides to take their guns when out with gentleman sportsmen, yet Old Bazil was an exception, as he always insisted on taking his. Around the camp-fire Dr. S---- spoke of his great wish to kill a caribou.

"Now," he said to old Bazil, "You bring me up close to one and I kill it, I'll give you a bonus of $10."

Several times next day during the still-hunt old Bazil would leave the doctor to await his return, while he would go forward reconnoitering carefully so there might be no mistake. At last he came back with the glad tidings to the doctor, that he had seen two caribou not far in advance of where they now were.

When it got to sneaking after Bazil through the last hundred yards to the few trees at the extreme edge of the forest, the doctor's heart was beating with such thumps that he thought the noise would start the game. The doctor at last reached the guide in the fringe of trees. Bazil told him that one of the deer was standing up, broadside on, while a little to the right was the second one lying down. The standing one being the larger of the two, and the only one having horns, was for the doctor to shoot, while the guide would take a pot-shot at the other. The doctor flattened out on his stomach and wriggled a few feet further, saw the deer through the branches, took aim and waited for Bazil to count the agreed one, two, three.

Bazil argued with himself that from the uncertain way the doctor's gun was wabbling about there were several hundred chances to one against his hitting the deer, and as a consequence, he would be minus his bonus.

So he employed a ruse. He counted the agreed signal to fire, but instead of firing at the one lying down, he drew a bead on the doctor's, and, of course, killed it.

At the report of the guns the caribou on the ground sprang up, and old Bazil, with consummate prevarication, said, "Oh! I missed it!" Aimed again, let go the other barrel, and killed this one also.

The doctor was wild with delight at his successful first shot, and expressed in many words his pleasure to old Bazil, who took it all in without a blush.

The old guide, who was standing up back of where the doctor fired, had taken no chance of missing with his smooth bore, but fired point blank at the deer's fore quarters. There was found on examination a frightful wound, and smashed bone; but the doctor was not versed enough in woodcraft to distinguish if this had been caused by a round bullet, and not the conical one from his own rifle.

The doctor was not a pot-hunter; he had what he came for, and had got it in almost record time, and was satisfied, so he fished for brook trout while Bazil carefully prepared the head for transportation and dried the meat for his own family. Then they journeyed back to Roberval, where the men were paid off, Bazil receiving a bright $10 gold piece as promised over and above his wages.

The doctor no doubt has that head, beautifully gotten up, hanging over his sideboard, and points to it with pride to his guests, saying, "I killed that head back of Kis-ki-sink, in Canada."

CHAPTER XXIII.

A CASE OF NERVE.

In the far interior where flour is scarce and our living consists of either fish or flesh, both of which we have to get when we can and how we can, the game laws are a dead letter. Nets were always in the water the year round and no one moved from the posts without a gun. Fish and potatoes were our staple diet and were it not for the abundance of the former we could never have lived in the country. Lakes were all about us and when one was fished out we moved our nets to another.

Flesh, however, could not always be got, and when the chance offered we killed, in season or out. Nothing, however, was wasted. Should we shoot a deer or moose in summer, the surplus over what we could consume in a day or two was either jerked and dried or salted. Many a time have my men had to visit our nets a mile or two off to get wherewith for our breakfast. If successful the fish had then to be cleaned and cooked before we broke our fast. Such being our hard battle for life I may be excused for the following story:

An Indian came in late one afternoon from his hunting grounds at the south to get his spring ammunition. It was about the middle of April and there was at the time a hard crust on the snow. He told us that on the way he had seen cuttings of a very big bull moose and he was sure he was on the top of a mountain near by where he had noticed the cuttings. He had no gun and besides the moose was useless to him so far from his camp being four or five miles from our post. Now he continued if you want to have him you can come along with me in the morning and you will surely kill him. He can't get away with the crust. The Indian was so sure of our success that he told me to take my two men with sleds to bring home the meat and hide.

As it was all ice walking except one short portage to the foot of the range of mountains he named, we decided to leave the post an hour or so before daylight so as to be there at the earliest possible moment. Our preparations were soon made and we took a little sleep dressed as we were and then started. We took two little partridge curs to head off the moose and keep him amused until I could catch up and shoot.

The hunt was going to be such a dead sure result that mine was the gun in the party. It was a smooth bore H. B. and carried bullets 28 to the pound. We had a cup of tea and a bite of galette at the foot of the mountain and left our sleds there together with the Indian's bundle of ammunition, tea, tobacco, etc., he had traded at the post. My men each carried one of the dogs in a bag to let go at the proper moment. As the Indian proposed in the first place to still hunt the bull, he reasoned that it being yet so early perhaps I would get a shot when he jumped up from his bed of the night.

We had to wear snow shoes in the green bush as the crust was not sufficient strong to support a man without them. We whipped strips of old rags about the frames to deaden the noise when walking on the hard snow. The Indian led off putting down each foot with the utmost care and I followed gun in hand the men being told to keep an acre or two behind us. The ascent was gradual and pretty free from undergrowth. We were getting near the summit when all at once the Indian called out, "he's off." After the stillness of our procedure these words were quite startling. The men heard him and hurried forward to us. The dogs were emptied out, they caught the tainted air in a moment and away they ran.

This was the first time I knew of an Indian's acute sense of smell, and after, when I came to consider it, could not think otherwise than that it was wonderful. From the place where we stood when he said, "The moose is away," was fully two acres to his lair, so it was impossible he could have seen or heard him go. In fact, he told me he smelt him when he sprang up. This I disbelieved at the time, but in after years had many instances that could not be doubted. Already the dogs were giving tongue down the descent on the other side and as they were barking apparently in the same place the moose was said to be at a standstill. The face of the mountain on the other side was wooded with a young growth of trees, in some places growing in thickets or clusters.

The Indian and the men followed me down hill and I approached the place where I heard the dogs, gun in hand. The dogs were, by the sound of their barking, running in on him and taking a nip at each run. After careful peering into the clump of trees I thought I made out his fore quarter and fired. The moose simply sat down and elevated his head until his neck appeared as long as that of a giraffe. I thought this was the forerunner of his tumbling over dead. This, however, was not the case, for the next minute he broke cover and charged straight for where I was standing, a distance of only a few yards. My companions turned and fled and I looked around for a suitable tree to dodge behind, but none was near. My left barrel was yet loaded and I realized my very life depended on my coolness and accurate shooting.

It takes considerable more time to write this down than the event itself took. I planted myself firmly on my snowshoes and waited the proper moment. All fear had passed and I fully realized it was death to me if I missed my shot. On he came his great eyes blazing green in his anger and the coarse hairs on his neck and shoulders standing up like quills. In a case of strong tension on the nerve like myself at that time moments appear hours. He was in the act of making his last spring before reaching me when I took a snap sight along the barrel and fired fair in the forehead. I had just time to step to one side when he fell dead right in my old tracks. Death had been so instantaneous that he was so to speak "killed on the fly." We skinned and cut up the meat and were back at the post before the midday thaw set in. It was only that night when I looked at the adventure from all points of view that I fully saw the great danger I had run.

CHAPTER XXIV.
AMPHIBIOUS COMBATS.

Very few of the present generation of hunters, I presume, have ever witnessed a fight between a beaver and an otter. I venture to think that the narrative of such an event will prove interesting to readers of *Hunter-Trader-Trapper*, especially as it comes first hand from the person who saw the fight from the start, and was in at the finish. It was an unique spectacle of once in thirty-five years of bush life.

I must digress a little at the start to explain that otters often, in the autumn, endeavor to find some tenantless beaver lodge situated on a chain of small lakes. If fortunate to find such, they at once pre-empt the old lodge and make it their home and headquarters. If the fish supply is ample in the lakes and small connecting creeks, they stay there until the snow hardens, and openings occur in the large rivers and then slide away to new fields, or rather, waterways. This migration is generally about the 20th of March in our Northern Country.

One day in the latter part of October I portaged my bark canoe over the divide into another chain of lakes, with the object of ascertaining if there were any beaver in that section. I came out to the shore of the lower lake of the string, in a small grassy bay, and was just in the act of taking the canoe off my head, when out in the bay, an acre or two from shore, I saw a beaver swimming on the surface at a high rate of speed. Being yet early in the afternoon I wondered at this and waited, with the canoe still tilted on my shoulders. All at once a long, shiny, snaky looking animal broke water in the wake of the beaver and a short distance behind the latter, evidently in pursuit.

The beaver was no sooner aware of this than he appeared actually to stand half out of the water, the next instant he turned and faced his pursuer. The distance between the two was so short that in a moment they were fast to each other's throat and then for some minutes neither could be seen for the churning and splashing of the water. I took the opportunity while they were thus engaged to unload my canoe and slip it half way into the lake ready to embark.

After the first fierce fighting impact and deadly grip, when they appeared pretty well exhausted — the fight going on at times on the surface — and again both would disappear beneath the waters of the lake, still locked together with the tenacity of bulldogs. Then they rose to the top, this time separated, and at some little distance apart, both plainly much spent. Then they circled about one another, much in the same way as two boxers sparring. Again a mad rush at each other, and again the strong jaws of his opponent, and the same scene was enacted again.

I thought it was about time to push out and take a closer aspect of affairs. The fight was interesting, but the chance of getting a beaver and an otter, with one shot, far surpassed the proverbial, "two birds with one stone."

What little breath of wind that ruffled the bay was in my favor, so with both barrels of my gun cocked leaning against the canoe bar, I sculled the birch silently but swiftly thru the water unnoticed by the combatants. When just about to take my gun, "the moment too late" occurred right then, and they separated as by mutual consent; the beaver swimming toward the shore and the otter pawing the water in a blind, dazed sort of a way. The latter being the nearer to the canoe and the most valuable of the two, I fired and killed him. On the flash and report of the gun, the beaver dived and I pushed the canoe in his direction, with the other barrel ready when he should come up. I had over-shot the place when he had disappeared and waited looking toward the shore, where I expected he would next come to view. Minutes passed and no sign, I turned about in the canoe thinking possibly he had doubled under. Not ten feet from the stern of the canoe, there was Mr. Beaver, dead without my firing a shot, dead from his wounds. I pulled him into the canoe and paddled back and picked up the otter.

After getting ashore and examining them both carefully and again when skinning them, I found the beaver had died of his terrible wounds and no doubt the otter was in the last throes of his life also, when I gave him his quittance. The hair and skin on their bellies were much scratched and cut up by the sharp, hard claws of their hind feet. Their necks were one mass of teeth marks, and the jugular veins in each were pierced. Both would have died of their wounds in a little while, without the use of the gun, had I withheld my fire for a few minutes, for they were fast bleeding to death.

I ascertained afterwards that this beaver had been the only one in the lake; the otter no doubt had driven him out of his house, and not content with this had pursued him, courting battle. In the fight that ensued, of which I had been a witness, both had met their death.

*   *   *   *   *

The sight I witnessed some years ago is so unique that I think it will prove interesting to the readers of *Forest and Stream*.

I was at the time stationed right in the moose country, having for its center the great Kipewa Lake. One day toward the end of November, when, as yet only the bays of the big lake were frozen, I started to visit some mink traps in my canoe, accompanied by a small little rat of a dog. It was still open water in the body of the lake, but as I have said, the bays were frozen a couple of inches thick. There is a long point of land jutting into the lake. Open water washed the beach on my side of this; but on the other side was a frozen bay. I landed about the middle of the point to fix up a mink trap. The little dog ran up into the timber, and a minute or two after I heard him giving tongue in a savage manner for so small a beast, and I knew he must have started up something extraordinary, possibly a bear. I ran down to the canoe for my gun, and started off in the direction of the barking, which by that time was becoming more remote. Pushing on, I came out to the shore on the opposite side of the point. Here I witnessed a sight never before nor after seen by me during a residence of over thirty years in the wilds of Canada.

A large cow moose was slipping about on the glare ice trying to make her way to the other side of the bay. I was so spellbound for a few moments that I let the opportunity pass to shoot. The ice was so glare that it was with difficulty the large animal could make headway at all.

My little dog had now come up with her, and very pluckily nipped her heels. The huge beast tried to turn in her headway to face the cur. In doing so, her four feet all slipped at once from under her, and her great weight coming down so suddenly on the thin ice caused it to break in fragments, and the moose was in the water.

To get out of that hole with no bottom to spring from was more than that moose, or any other, could do, but the poor beast did not realize this, and continued swimming around, and every now and again getting its front hoofs on the slippery edge, only to fall backward again into the icy waters.

The dog followed it about the opening, barking continually, but the moose had more pressing business than to bother with a small dog. I saw that the creature would never succeed in extracting itself, and thought to end its misery. From where I stood the distance from the shore was about two hundred yards. I therefore started to load my gun (it was before the days of breechloaders), but when I got to the final of putting on the percussion cap, there was none.

Although I was positively sure the moose would be frozen stiff in that hole in the morning, the fascination of the sight kept me standing there on the rocks watching her struggles.

I must have stood there for two full hours, as the sun of the short November day began to get near the treetops, and a cold, cutting north wind began to blow.

The poor moose was now swimming about very slowly, and at times turning up on her side. This told me the end was not far off.

The last look I gave she had part of her head resting on the ice, and her body was floating on its side. Then I recrossed the point and paddled home as fast as I could.

Next morning we got a large canoe out of winter quarters, and with my two men we paddled back to the point, supplied with ropes and axes. The night had been a cold one, and had increased the thickness of the ice sufficient for us to walk upon. We cut a couple of long pines, or levers, and went out to the hole. The head was frozen just in the position I had last seen it, and this kept the body from sinking. Our first precaution was to chop the ice away about the carcass and get ropes about it. Then we got another around the neck and chopped the head clear.

We dropped it as it was to the shore, and there cut it up in quarters. All of the breast, neck and front legs were quite useless, being a mass of conjected blood and bruised flesh, caused by the moose's contact with the ice. These condemned parts, however, were not altogether useless, because I used them to bait my traps. Besides the eatable part of the meat, I got twenty pairs of shoes out of the hide.

*   *   *   *   *

Just after the above account of the very unusual occurrence was received, a press dispatch telling of a somewhat similar happening appeared in the New York newspapers. There is no doubt that accidents of one sort and another are responsible for the death of large game much more frequently than we imagine. It is certain also that among the young of such animals there is a considerable mortality, although we do not know that any observations on this subject have been recorded. Every man who has hunted much, however, has probably seen something of this, and we should be glad to record any such experiences of this sort which our readers have had. We ourselves have not infrequently found young deer and antelope that had evidently died from diseases, and more seldom have seen young elk, and on two occasions, young mountain sheep, dead, for whose taking off there seemed to be no reason to be advanced except sickness. It is well known that on the fur seal islands of the North Pacific and the Bering Sea, thousands of pups die annually from disease, in addition to the vastly greater number which starve to death through the killing of the mothers by pelagic sealing.

The *Sun* account above referred to reads as follows:

Captains Wisner, Verity and Ira Udall, who have been across the bay to Fire Island beach, arrived here to-day. They say that two deer, one a fine large six-year-old buck and the other a doe, had walked out on the ice and had broken through. They had been unable to get back to the mainland and were carried with the current. They drifted across the bay a distance of nearly ten miles and were being taken out into the ocean when seen by Captains Udall and Verity from the State wharf east of the lighthouse.

The two men put off in a lifeboat and succeeded in driving the buck ashore. The doe was almost dead by that time. Every effort was made to get her ashore and save her life. A rope was fastened around her body and she was soon on shore, although after no little effort. She soon, however, died of exhaustion. The buck ran off east on the beach, but unless its instinct is strong enough to teach it to follow the beast east to the mainland, seventy miles distant, it will soon starve, as the sand hills and meadows are now bare of vegetation.

CHAPTER XXV.
ART OF PULLING HEARTS.

I see by inquiries answered and letters from F. Edgar Brown in an issue of Hunter-Trader-Trapper that my casual mention of pulling the heart of the fox in "Reynard Outwitted," has struck a chord of interest with trappers. As the knack of pulling the hearts of the smaller animals trapped is worth knowing, and will save the hunter dirty work in the skinning of the pelts, I will describe the process as plain as I can.

It is bad enough to skin an animal that has been struggling in a steel trap, and got the imprisoned leg a mass of congealed blood, without adding to the disagreeableness of the job crushing in his head or breaking his back with a pole. This at least can be avoided by pulling down the heart till the cords snap. In no other way do Indians, or those who have learned trapping from Indians, kill the small animals they find alive when visiting their line of traps. Foxes, martens, minks and rabbits are always killed in this way. Lynx, of course, is a nasty animal to approach in a trap, still the Indian trapper never thinks of shooting, or hitting him with a pole. On the contrary they fix a noosed cord to a young sapling cut for the purpose, and snare him from the length of the pole; once over his head they stand on the pole and let him struggle till dead. This prevents blood from being on the skin. A live bear in a steel trap must be shot to make "a good bear of him."

But the Indian trapper again uses his judgment and waits till the first violent struggles are over, and the bear somewhat quiet, then the hunter takes careful aim and puts a bullet into his ear, being always at pretty close range. The ball passes clear thru the head, killing the bear instantly and making a wound that bleeds profusely, so that when the skinning process takes place, there is no blood in the body. The skin is cut around the throat, skinned towards the body and the head left as it is. However, this is digressing from the subject at issue.

The small animals I have mentioned when caught with snow on the ground, are simply walked on top of by the hunter's snowshoes; once he is pinned down so that he cannot move, the trapper slips his left hand under snowshoes and secures the fox or whatever it is by the neck with a tight grip of the thumb and fingers. Then the snowshoe is withdrawn until it holds the hind quarters only; the hand with the head and neck is elevated until the body is extended to its utmost.

The right hand now feels for the heart just below the bottom rib; it may not be there at once, but it will come. When the animal feels the grip tightening on his throat the sense of strangulation causes the heart to jump down and up in the body in the most violent manner. This the hunter seizes at one of the downward pumps, catches it between the thumb and fingers of the right hand; then pulling the body in one direction and the heart in the other, the heart-strings snap. The animal gives a convulsive quiver and you chuck him down dead.

Oh yes! it is much better than the brutal way of banging them on the head with the axe handle or a pole, and much more humane because the animal is dead at once, almost as quick as if shocked with electricity. Animals trapped in the late fall, or early snow, cannot be held by the snowshoe, therefore some other means must be taken. It does not do to take any risks of being bitten, for animals after struggling in a trap for some time, become more or less mad, consequently the venom getting into one's blood might cause a very bad wound to heal, especially as the man who hunts cannot avoid the cold getting into the sore, and then should such happen one cannot foretell what the sequel may be.

To avoid therefore all mishaps the hunter draws his belt axe, and cuts a forked young birch or alder, the handle part being about four feet long, at the extremity of which a fork is left with prongs of five or six inches long.

Presenting this to the trapped beast, he snaps at it; the trapper watches his chance and deftly slips the fork over his neck and with a quick downward push, marten, fox or fisher is secured. The left hand is exchanged for the forked stick, the right foot is placed on his hind quarters to keep him from clawing, then go for his heart with the right hand. One trying for the first time may have some little difficulty, but after a few animals have passed thru his hands he will as well as I do, know the ART OF PULLING HEARTS.

During my many years as a fur trader, part of the time has been passed on the frontier where opposition is keen and hunters, both Indians and whites, are careless in preparing their peltries for market. As long as they are dried in a way to keep, is all sufficient for them. Musquash will be simply drawn over a bent willow and dried in the blazing sun or near the camp fire. The little animal is hastily skinned and considerable fat is left on the skin, which, by being subjected to a quick and great heat, penetrates the skin and it is consequently grease burnt.

The greater number of beaver skins one gets about the Canadian villages are badly gotten up. This, in a great measure, is due to the French custom of buying by weights instead of by the skin, the hunters reasoning that the more meat, grease, flippers, etc., they can leave on, the greater number of pounds gross.

Mink and otter are the two hardest animals we have to skin clean, and the majority we get on the frontier go to the London markets in a shameful state, and must tend towards their decrease in value. I have seen foxes, minks, martens and musquash as taken crumpled like rags from the same bag. It was a great wrench for me after handling skins of every sort positively prime, and as clean as the paper upon which this is printed, for twenty years to find myself on the frontier buying such burnt and crumpled skins, as I found was the rule rather than the exception.

Yes, it was a pleasure to barter the furs hunted by our inland Indians; every skin was brought to the post hair side in. If the Indian had a bear, the two flanks were turned in lengthwise of the skin, then the hide was folded twice, the thick part of the head and shoulders being brought down on top of all as a protection to the thinner parts. Large beaver were folded crosswise of the skin twice, making a kind of portfolio about eighteen inches wide by twenty-eight to thirty inches long. Small beaver were folded once lengthwise of the skin, and these came to us as a rule, two placed inside of each large beaver as they went.

In the interior where the hunters have well defined grounds to trap on they, by self-interest, protect the beaver and kill comparatively few young ones. Our average for the whole year would probably be one small one to two middle or full grown. The martens are tied flat the whole length of the skins in bundles of ten each, with a thin splinter of cedar wood on top and bottom to prevent them from being crumpled in any way. Minks are treated just as carefully. Foxes, fisher and lynx are folded one crosswise and then placed either inside of beaver or bear skins. Thus nothing is exposed from an Indian's pack of furs, either to view or friction, but strong leather. Musquash, like all other skins except bear and beaver, are skinned from the head down and each skin is cased, which makes them clean, flat and nice to handle.

As their hunts are made during the cold months when the animals have their primest coats, and as every particle of flesh or grease is frost scraped, the skin lastly washed on the case and then the pelt dried by the action of frost alone, it can be readily understood with such care as I have tried to explain, that we get the very finest and most pleasing skins that go out of the country. The Indian's business is to hunt and bring the fruits of the chase or traps to his wigwam; it is his wife and daughters' duty to skin and cure the pelts. The Indians have the pride and ambition to vie with their sister matrons of the forest as to who will get up the cleanest, best and "well prepared skins."

CHAPTER XXVI.

DARK FURS.

It is not perhaps generally known that the surroundings of most animals have a primary effect on the color of their hair. Beaver, otter, mink and musquash are dark or light colored according to the water they live in. Clear, cold water lakes produce skins of a deep glossy black, muddy lakes on the other hand, furnishing light colored fur.

Having studied this in my own hunting and trapping, I have often surprised an Indian when trading his skins by saying: "You trapped this and this skin in a clear water lake," and he has admitted it as true. Another peculiar fact in relation to deep, cold water lakes is that, while the skins they produce are of the finest quality, they are also much smaller in size than those trapped in brown or muddy water, and this applies to all the animals I have mentioned.

Musquash killed in clear water lakes are about two-thirds the size of those trapped in grassy, sluggish rivers, and it is the same with mink. This rule holds good also with land animals, such as marten, those living in and resorting to black spruce swamps being invariably dark colored, whereas those in mixed pine, birch and balsam hills are larger and lighter in color.

For seven years I trapped on a chain of lakes, five in number. One of these lay off at one side, not over a quarter of a mile from the other four; it was of considerable extent, possibly a mile and a half long by a quarter wide. This lake was very clear and deep, and used to freeze over two weeks later than the others, and open that much earlier in the spring.

On the borders of this lake, which was known as "Clear Water Lake," were two beaver lodges, which I preserved with the greatest care, only trapping a few out of each lodge every fall, thus keeping up the supply, and finer and more beautiful skins I never handled. This valley being within a few miles of the post, I got the Indian who owned the lands to make over his rights for a consideration, and I kept these lakes as a home farm or preserve as long as I remained in that district.

It was in the upper one of these lakes that I trapped the most extraordinary beaver of my experience, he having only one hind foot, the other feet having been gnawed or twisted off in traps. The Indian owner of the lands, when selling his good will, told me of this desperate and cunning old animal and I passed many a long, solitary evening in my canoe to get a shot when the knowing old card broke water.

I kept two or three traps well set, with a very remote possibility of his putting his only remaining foot therein. Beaver medicine and castorum would not allure him, and the thought occurred to me to try anise seed oil, which I did, and on my next visit had the satisfaction of pulling him up drowned at the end of the chain. The wounds of the cut off legs were so thoroughly healed that when I skinned him there was not even a pucker of the skin in the places where the legs should have been. It is a marvel how he managed to navigate the waters of his native pond, but as the boy said, "I don't know how he did it, but he did."

Another freak that I caught in those same lakes was the only albino beaver that I ever saw. She had a creamy white fur, with pink eyes, pink toe nails and pink scales on her tail. This may not have been phenomenal, but it was a rare skin for all that. At a conservative estimate I must have handled a couple hundred thousand beaver skins in my life, but this is the only instance that I ever saw a white one.

The Clear Water Lake, not to be behind in oddities, produced a dwarf beaver. I caught him late in the fall in a trap set for musquash, the other lakes being frozen over. He was about the size of an ordinary full grown rat, but was fully developed and must have been two years old. At first I thought he might be of a second litter, but I thought this was very improbable, if not quite outside of nature, so I carefully examined the teeth and organs, and found to intents and purposes he was a full grown beaver.

Writing of full grown beaver puts me in mind of those early trapping days, and the logic of a certain Indian. Then we used to pay so much a skin for beaver, and graded the skins as big, middling and small. In culling this man's skins I threw one into the pile of middling ones and he immediately said: "That's a big one," and I said it was not and compared it with several of the large ones. He, however, stoutly maintained it was a big one and said, "Look at the white men, there are big ones and small ones, but they are men the same." I stood corrected and placed the disputed skin with his better grown and developed relatives, the Indian gave an almost audible smile, and things went on amicably.

On the watershed between the valley of the St. Lawrence and Hudson's Bay, marten are prime on the first of October. Beaver, otter and mink are prime on the 25th of October and fox and lynx the 15th of November. I have often seen the question asked in the H-T-T as to the time the several kinds of fur are prime in different localities, and the above dates can be depended upon for the latitude mentioned.

It pays the trapper to have his trap-houses made and his traps hung up ready to set and bait immediately when the skins are prime. They are easily cleaned and command a much higher average, whereas if the majority of skins in a man's pack are unprimed or staged, it takes away from the value of the few really few good ones.

The buyer, to get these few merchantable skins, has to put some kind of value on the culls to make a buy, but in reality the trader is only paying for the few good ones and the trapper loses the other skins. And who is to blame? Trappers have been told time and again that trapping too early in the season is against their best interests; nevertheless they go blindly on, killing the poor beasts that have little or no value, and then they marvel at the scarcity of the fur-bearing animals and the little return they have to show for a couple of months' hard work.

No. If there is any line that wants protection and a cast iron union between the men connected with the industry, it is the fur trade. All are, or ought to be, interested in the keeping up of the supply and quality, the trapper, wholesale man and manufacturer alike. Let the last two unite and not buy unprime skins, and the former for want of a market would very soon hunt in season only.

*   *   *   *   *

In this northern country fur-bearing animals continue prime much longer than elsewhere. The trappers and hunters (Indians) only come down from the interior from the tenth of June, and all the way down to the end of the month. Thus the month of June is the fur buying month.

Prior to the Paris Exposition a fair and legitimate trade was possible, the Indians got a fair and reasonable price for their skins, and as a rule were reasonably honest. But that year marked the demoralization of the fur trade on this coast. Opposition became keen and fur buyers from Quebec, Boston, New York and Paris, came to the different places of resort of the Indians, bidding up raw furs to prices out of all reason. The consequence of which were, and are, that the Indian did not pay his furnisher, but kept up his finest furs to sell to these parties for high cash prices.

Other traders followed the fur buyers, and sold the Indians useless trashy articles. The result is the Indians have to leave for the bush ill supplied with warm clothings, provisions, etc. — what he actually requires. A large portion of his hunt has been sold for abnormal prices, but the proceeds has done him no perceptible good. On the contrary, his lot is much worse than it was before. Seeing his advances have not been paid, the resident trader will not supply these men again.

I take about the Post of Seven Islands as perhaps being the place where the highest prices have been paid for three years, 1899, 1900 and 1901, and give the readers of Hunter-Trader-Trapper the figures. They are as follows:

Bears, large, black from	$15.00	to	$25.00
Bears, small, black, from	6.00	to	12.00
Beaver per lb.	3.50	to	4.50
Fisher, from	6.00	to	10.00
Fox, red, from	3.50	to	5.50
Fox, cross, from	4.00	to	25.00
Fox, silver, from	100.00	to	335.00
Lynx, from	4.00	to	7.00
Marten, from	10.00	to	20.00
Minks, from	2.50	to	4.00
Otters, land, from	15.00	to	22.00

Wolverine, from   4.00 to 6.00

These are the principal furs we have on the Coast and will show what absurd prices were paid. We know that furs realized good prices at the last London sales, and some few, very few, bought were no doubt well worth these high prices.

The part where the most harm was done the trade was the anxiety of some of these buyers to get the furs at almost any price. Almost any kind of a marten would be paid $10 for. Such martens that the writer of this article has bought a few years ago for $1.25, a very choice marten, large, dark and well furred, one we will say out of two or three hundred, such a one as we ordinarily paid $7 for, has brought $18 to $20. Martens and otters especially, they seem to have gone perfectly crazy to get.

Two years ago a man, further down the Coast paid $720 for what I was told was a very ordinary Silver Fox. He went to Paris during the Exposition with the fox to sell. I never heard if he got his money back. Had he paid $150, he would have got the fox just the same for this was the price being paid along the Coast during that year.

The rivers are the highways of the Indians and the mouths of most of the big ones are the summer camping grounds. At these places are trading posts where they barter and sell their winter's catch, get new supplies for another year, and load their canoes again in September for another nine or ten months in the Far North Wilds.

When the reaction comes, as it must come, it will be pretty hard to convince the Indians that their martens are only worth $5 or $6. The bottom is bound to fall out, and many of these men, who are paying the present prices, must go to the wall. With unlimited money, any fool can buy skins. But it requires a judge and careful man to buy with discretion.

CHAPTER XXVII.
INDIANS ARE POOR SHOTS.

During a residence of many years among four different tribes of Indians, I found, with very few exceptions, they were poor shots, either with the gun or rifle.

When one considers that from young boyhood they have been in the habit of using a gun almost daily, and their very living depends, in great manner, on accurate shooting, their poor marksmanship is to be wondered at, nevertheless such is the case. A good wing shot is a rarity among the Indians.

The Montagnais of the Labrador and North Shore of the Gulf of St. Lawrence, are no exception, and this in a country where most of the wild fowl are killed flying. It is admitted they kill wild geese and ducks while on their passage north and south, but this is only possible from the immense numbers of birds and a lavish expenditure of ammunition.

It is a common thing for an Indian getting his spring outfit to go among the islands to take from the trader one hundred pounds of shot, a keg of twenty-five pounds of powder and two thousand five hundred percussion caps (they use muzzleloaders). They always take about 20 per cent. more caps than are necessary to fire the powder, as they explain, to make up for what they drop.

The Indians are very partial to loon; but, as a rule, it is the most expensive food they eat. A great number alight on Lake Ka-ke-bon-ga on their way north in the spring. This happens about the time the Indians arrive at the Post to trade their winter catch of furs.

When a poor unfortunate loon would settle on the lake it was the signal for ten or twenty canoes to put off and shoot or drown him to death. Far more frequently, I fancy, the poor bird expired from want of air than weight of shot.

To watch these loon hunts from the gallery of our house was picturesque in the extreme, the canoes going, some in one direction as fast as the paddlers could drive them, and then all of a sudden the cry would ascend that the loon had broken water in quite the opposite place from where they were confident he would. Then in a moment, the canoes would be whirled about like tops, and off again in the new direction, possibly to again find they are at fault.

The wonder to me was there were no casualties, as almost incessant firing was kept up, with canoes going in several directions at once, and all on the save level; and when the loon would emerge, bang! would go several guns, regardless where pointed, in the excitement.

I call to memory one day in particular. At the call of "loon!" I took a seat on the gallery, with the fixed resolve to count how many shots would be fired, and this is the result of my tab.

Twelve canoes put off from the camps, four hours consumed in the killing, and ninety-six shots were fired.

This happened nearly forty years ago, when powder sold, at that inland post, at a dollar a pound; shot, thirty-three cents, and gun caps a half a cent each, so the reader can readily see that loon meat, under that way of hunting, was expensive.

We read of and are told about the great slaughter the Indians used to make among the buffalo in the good old days; but this success was not to be attributed to their good marksmanship, because they killed these noble beasts with their guns almost "boute touchant."

One thing about their mode of loading and firing might be interesting to readers of the present day, inasmuch as a generation has been born and has grown up since the last buffalo roamed the plains.

The Indians and half-breeds who went on these periodical round-ups were armed with and preferred the old nor-west muzzle-loading flint-lock. They could load and fire with such rapidity that one would almost fancy they carried a repeating gun. Suspended under their right arm by a deer thong, was a common cow's horn of powder, and in a pouch at their belt a handful or two of bullets.

As the horse galloped up to the herd, the Indian would pour a charge of powder into his left hand, transfer it into the barrel of the gun, give the butt a pound on the saddle, and out of his mouth drop on top a bullet. As the lead rolled down the barrel it carried in its wet state particles of powder that stuck on the sides, and settled on top of the powder charge. No rod or ramming was used.

The gun was carried muzzle up, resting on the hollow of left arm until such time as the Indian desired to fire. The quarry being so close no aim was required. On deflecting the barrel the trigger was pulled before the ball had time to roll clear of the powder.

The Indians saw that their buffalo guns had very large touch-holes, thereby assuring the pan being primed. When all the balls were fired a few others were chuked into the mouth, and merrily went the game.

No! The Indians are not good shots.

CHAPTER XXVIII.

A BEAR IN THE WATER.

The bear has one trait especially that is most dangerous to the uneducated hunter, and that is when found swimming a lake or river he invariably goes in a straight line from where he left the shore. Any obstacle in the way he clambers over, be it a log, boat or canoe.

Should the place where he reaches the further shore be a high rocky bluff, he climbs this, rather than turn from his direct course. This may be pigheadedness or stupidity; be it as it may, he will not turn to a low-shelving beach a few yards at one side, but it never enters his head to take the easier landing.

I once saw a bear swimming across near the discharge of a lake. There was a string of booms hanging down stream near the other shore and at right angles to where he was heading. He simply clambered over the boom logs and took the water again on the other side, instead of trotting along the boom to the shore.

I was acquainted with an old Indian, who, knowing this trait of bears to land where they head for, did a deed of great nerve for a man of over sixty. He was visiting his fish net on the shore of a narrow lake, when he saw a large bear enter the water on the opposite side a little above, and head for the shore the old man was on. Old Pete had no gun, but he did not hesitate a moment, but caught up his hunting ax, and ran along shore to where the bear would land. The old man was plainly visible to the bear from the first, but Bruin kept on his direct course. Old Pete waded out from the shore nearly to his waist with ax unlifted, and waited. Everything depended on striking true, and at the proper and precise moment. He had the bear, it is true, at a disadvantage. Still, many a younger and stronger man would have declined the risk.

Pete was successful; he buried the ax clean into the skull the first blow.

Another instance I witnessed of a bear not turning aside for any obstacle: We were later than usual one evening on the water; my men were anxious to get to the portage before camping, and were tracking the canoe up the last mile at deep dusk. There were four men on the line ashore, and the bow and steersmen standing up in the canoe fending her off the rocks and shallows. My companion and I were sitting very quietly in the middle compartment of our large canoe; the men also were not in a talking mood, being tired and hungry. I was sitting on the side next the river and noticed a black object which at first I mistook for a stone, partly out of the water; but with a second, and more searching look, I made it out to be a bear coming straight toward the canoe.

I gave warning to the man in the bow, who stood a few feet in front of me, and he immediately gave a sharp tug on the tow line, which checked the men ashore. The bear by this time was about five or six yards from the canoe, and just opposite me. I saw that nothing would now stop him from climbing into and across the canoe. Before he could place his paw on the side of the bark the man in the bow made a savage lunge at him with his pike pole, but before he could give a second blow the bear was in on my side and out on the other, right across our legs. Our men of the tow had run back, the man in the stern being too far off to be of any use, had the presence of mind to throw an armful of paddles, which being of maple, made formidable weapons. When the bear got out on the shore side they rained blows upon blows with the sharp blades of the paddles upon his head and body as they could get a chance. The bow man sprang ashore and lent his assistance with his formidable pole, but marvelous as it may sound, the bear escaped into the bush in spite of all that his assailants could do to prevent him.

Long into the night about the dying embers of the camp-fire, I heard the men going over the whole scene and blaming one another for not having done something they ought to have done.

One other instance I will give of a bear's persistency to go straight in the water, and in this case it was fatal to two men.

Two newly married couples left the mouth of the Moisie for the interior. Their third day up stream brought them to a place where, off to one side in the bush about a mile back, was a noted lake for trout and whitefish. It was decided that they should portage one canoe, and with their blankets, net and cooking utensils go and pass the night on the lake shore. One gun was all the men took (a flintlock — for this was years ago). Shortly after arriving at the lake a bear was seen swimming from the other side, coming toward where the Indians were tying their net. The two young men jumped into the canoe and pushed out to meet him, which was a fatal mistake. The man in the bow waited till the bear was within a couple of yards off from the bow, and then pulled the trigger. The old gun flashed in the pan, but there was no report. The next instant the bear clambered over the head of the canoe and rolled the occupants into the water. The young brides of a few days ran screaming along shore, unable to render any assistance to their husbands, and actually witnessed both drown before their very eyes.

I remember the arrival of the two poor women back to the coast, and the relation of their pathetic story. To make the case much more remarkable, they were twins by birth, and twin widows by this tragedy.

A word of advice after the foregoing illustrations of the danger of getting in front of a swimming bear is hardly now necessary, but one cannot impress too forcibly the danger in attacking a bear by a frontal move. Always approach a bear in the water either on one side or from the rear. You can paddle up quite close to a bear in the direction he is swimming without the least particle of danger, and a more vital and telling spot to fire at cannot be got than the back and base of the skull.

CHAPTER XXIX.

VORACIOUS PIKE.

Calling the pike the fresh water shark is a name well applied, for he is bold and anything that comes his way is food for his maw. It is a known fact to those who have studied its habits that he will eat frogs, young ducks, musquash, in fact, anything that happens to be in front of him, not even barring his own offspring. How destructive they are in a trout or whitefish lake is well known.

One of the lakes on which I was stationed years ago was said to have been, formerly, good for whitefish, but was now almost nude of this staple food of the dwellers at the post, brought about by the increasing number of pike.

As I was likely to be in charge, for a few years at least, I set to work to destroy these marauders. The lake is only a mile and a half long by a quarter broad. It discharges into a large river by a shallow creek, but, by this creek, no doubt, many pike were added to the number at each spawning time.

The creek took my attention first, and we staked it from side to side with pickets six feet high and planted them about two inches apart.

At the back or river side of this barrier we kept some old, almost useless, nets set continuously. They were doubled so that no small sized pike could pass. This was done during the low water in August.

My next move was to employ every boy, girl and old woman about the post trolling for pike. We supplied them with the trolls and lines and paid them a cent apiece for every pike over a foot long.

During this trolling process we kept some nets of large mesh, set purposely for the bigger ones. For days and weeks there must have been landed on an average a hundred a day, and yet they came.

As most of the pay was taken out in cheap "bullseyes" at a cent apiece, the real outlay in money was not considerable.

The following spring we inaugurated another system of warfare against the pests, and that was by paddling quietly around the bays and shooting them while they lay spawning and basking in the sun and shallow water.

Often three or four would be clustered together. A shot would not kill the whole, but it would stun them so we could finish them with the paddle.

One that was killed in this way measured thirty-nine inches long and weighed thirty-five pounds. A fish of this size was good eating, and therefore used at the post.

The small, slimy ones, however, were burned in numbers on a brush heap.

With such persistent and continued onslaught on our part, at the end of the first year their numbers were very noticeably decreased, and at the close of the following summer they were positively scarce, and a very welcome number of whitefish stocked our lake in their place.

I resided at that post for twelve years, and we were never in want of the finest fish for the post's consumption.

Before closing this sketch I must tell one anecdote about a pike, even if I lay myself open to be disbelieved by the reader. I am well aware that fish stories stand in bad repute and the veracity of the narrator doubted. The following is positively true and came under my notice:

Years before the foregoing part of my story happened I was stationed on the height of land north of Lake Superior, and one afternoon portaged my canoe over into a small chain of beaver lakes hunting for signs.

It was a "still, calm day," as some high-flown writer would put it.

A feather dropped would have fallen straight to the earth.

I was paddling very quietly out into the lake from the portage when I noticed something moving very gently on the surface a few yards ahead of the canoe. Getting closer I made this out to be the fin of some fish moving sluggishly. Pushing the canoe further in advance with noiseless knife strokes of the paddle, I got close enough to see it was a pike with a whitefish half protruding from its mouth and almost dead from suffocation.

This, I thought, is a rare occurrence for a person to witness, and gently reaching out my hand I inserted my thumb and finger into the eye sockets and lifted both into the canoe.

On getting ashore at the next portage I forced open the jaws of the pike, and the whitefish dropped from them. The half that had been inside the pike's mouth was quite decomposed, while the part out in the water was comparatively fresh.

In trying to swallow this fish, which was two-thirds the pike's own length, he had distended his jaws to the utmost, but they only opened enough to reach near the back fin, and here fixing his teeth in savage fury the biter had bitten more than he could eat. He was equally unable to disgorge himself as he was incapable of swallowing, and thus by his greediness he brought on his doom.

Noticing his stomach was in a distended shape caused me to rip it open with my knife, and out tumbled the remains of a smaller whitefish, almost quite digested, which had been swallowed whole and would have measured nearly a foot long.

It was gluttony and not hunger that caused him to reach an untimely end, a moral for greedy little boys.

CHAPTER XXX.
THE BRASS-EYED DUCK.

The whistler, whistle-wing, great head, garrot or brass-eyed is one of the few ducks that, to my knowledge, builds its nest in trees.

The Indians, who are noted for giving appropriate names, call this duck "arrow duck," on account of its quick passage through the air. They fly very swiftly, and it is only an expert gunner that can bring them down in succession.

I once had the rare opportunity of watching the doings of a female brass-eyed from the building of the nest to the time she placed the young ones on the waters of the lake. To watch the industrious little builder was a most interesting pastime and afforded me much pleasure. The tree selected was not, as one would suppose, immediately on the shore, but a bit back in the thick growth. Properly speaking, the tree was a stump, although a strong live one grew rubbing sides with it. The stump was on the south side of the green one, and thus protected from the north, and was about twenty feet in height.

On examination shortly after the duck began to lay, I found that the concave top had been lined with dead leaves, hay, clay and small sticks. After this one peep in at the architecture and the couple of eggs therein, I refrained from approaching the stump again, but continued my observations from a distance.

When the duck took to steady setting I could just see her head and bill over the edge of the nest. Regularly each evening during the period of incubation she would fly out onto the lake to feed, drink and plume herself. These absences from her duty lasted from twenty minutes to half an hour.

When the young were hatched I kept a strict and steady watch on her movements for the thought occurred to me, "How would they get to the ground?" But, like a good many other things, this riddle of the forest was made clear to me one evening near sundown.

I sat motionless in my canoe a little to one side of the direction of the stump. The lake was as calm as oil, and in a little while, after taking up my position, out flew the mother in a slanting way to the water, and hanging from her bill was one of the young ducks. This she quickly deposited on the lake and flew back to the nest, and made trips to and fro, until she had brought the whole of her brood which numbered seven.

A hen is a proud mother even with one chick; well this was a transported one with seven. She swam through the midst of them, around them, away from them and toward them, exhibiting the utmost delight. Finally she led them in toward the shore, the shadows of the woods shutting them out from further observation. While daily visiting my nets about the lake, I often encountered the brood, or saw them at a short distance and they continued to interest me.

One day the number of ducklings appeared fewer than ought to be and on counting them I found there were only five. Next day this was reduced to four, and a few days after, when next I saw them, there remained only three. However, the mystery of their disappearance was made clear to me on that same day, for while trolling past the ducks' feeding grounds a big maskinonge struck the hooks savagely.

Being alone in the frail and small canoe I had the utmost difficulty to successfully play and kill him, but was amply paid, for on cleaning the big fish we found in its maw one of my young ducks.

Thus was their mysterious disappearance explained, this, or some other large fish, was accountable for the brood's diminution.

While on the subject of the brass-eye I would wish to set the reader right in regard to the whistling noise they make, that is the male. The author of "Wild Fowl and Their Habits" asserts that this noise is made by their short sharp wings cutting the air in rapid flight. Were this the case the female would make the same sound, but no one ever heard this whistling from a lone female or a number of females.

It is from the male we get this; not from the wings, however, but from a gristly sac attached at the end of the wind-pipe, much the shape of the bag of the bagpipes. From this he emits several different kinds of sounds, as I have often listened to when approaching a flock on a calm moonlight night in the mating season.

Another erroneous assertion by the same author is that the flesh is rank, fishy and hard. The old ones are, more or less so, on their first arrival inland in the spring. At the sea, as a necessity, they live on fish, but a month after reaching inland waters, where they feed on marine plants and roots, the color of the flesh changes. It also becomes juicy and is as good eating as black duck or teal.

The young ones, when full fledged, just before migrating to the sea for the winter, are excellent.

The French-Canadians call this duck the diver and the half-breeds of Hudson Bay the pork duck.

All the tricks of hiding attributed to this duck by Netlje Blanchan, author of the book from which I have taken the several names under which the duck is known to American readers, are quite true, and also other devices not enumerated. For instance, when wounded I have known it to dive and come up within a few yards of my canoe with its head under a water-lily leaf and there remain, quite motionless, until I noticed the center elevation of this single leaf and fired at a venture with the result that I killed the duck.

On another occasion I noticed a wounded brass-eye making toward the shore in very shallow water. The formation of the banks was such that it was impossible for it to land and hide. Nevertheless, toward that shore it had dived, and never appeared above water. Pushing the canoe quietly along with my gun ready in the other hand, I scanned every inch as I went. Along the beach there was a solution of mud almost as light as the water. The duck had passed under this and came to the shore in about five inches of water showing nothing but its bill on the beach, the entire body being covered with mud, the exact counterpart of that about it.

Although my canoe was within six feet of the bird, it never moved, and it was only by the closest scrutiny that I detected its presence.

With a good silent dog playing in front of a blind these ducks in the early spring will come within short range, as will the black duck and gray goose. They have keen eyesight and will work in from a quarter of a mile to investigate the dog. The dog of best color to attract ducks is yellow or yellow and white. A pure white is better than a dark colored, which latter only appears to scare them away.

[This is an interesting contribution, for it brings up a number of points about which there has been more or less controversy in the past, and one at least which is new to us. That Mr. Hunter's duck brought her young to the water in her bill is interesting and agrees with statements made years ago in *Forest and Stream* by Mr. George A. Boardman, who quoted a Canadian informant as stating that the old birds brought their young from the nests to the water, carrying them in their bills, but that to transport the young for a longer distance, the birds carried the young pressed to the body by the feet, a description which is not altogether clear.

Mr. Hunter declares that the whistling noise made by the brass-eye does not come from the wings and that this noise is never made by the female, in this his opinion differs from that of many other writers. In his belief the labyrinth — an enlargement of the wind-pipe found in the male of most ducks and but seldom in the female — explains the whistling sound so commonly heard when these birds fly near us.

Food notoriously gives flavor to the flesh of ducks as well as other animals. On the sea coast, where it feeds on fish and perhaps shell fish, the flesh of the brass-eye or golden-wing is notoriously bad, but like Mr. Hunter, other authors have declared that inland the bird is excellent eating.

The observation of the destruction of the brood by the maskinonge is worth recording. Pike, pickerel, maskinonge and snapping turtles are notorious enemies of young duck.]

CHAPTER XXXI.

GOOD WAGES TRAPPING.

I questioned a couple of hunters (brothers) this summer, as to the results of their hunting adventures of the past season, and as I wanted to find out their positive net gains, I got the following figures from them.

They are just fairly good trappers and their success is about what two industrious men could do who had a knowledge of trapping. Their work was in two spells. Three months in the fall and early winter and a month and a half in spring.

The provisions they took inland for the three months (ascending one of the North Shore rivers) was the following with costs given: 160 lbs. pork, $20.00; 20 lbs. butter, $3.00; 360 lbs. flour, $6.40; 6 lbs. tea, $2.10; 24 lbs. sugar, $1.20; 2 lbs. soda, 10 cts.; salt and pepper, 20 cts.; $33.00.

Their canoe was pretty well laden when they left the coast, inasmuch as besides the foregoing gross weight of provisions their outfit of tent, axes, pots, kettles, guns, tracking line, poling irons, four dozen No. 1 traps, half dozen No. 3 and a quarter dozen No. 5 bear had to be added to the load, bringing the total weight approximately up to seven hundred and fifty pounds.

Even when a canoe is loaded and, at times, overloaded, yet there are a number of incidentals that have to be taken along, things that weigh and are bulky, yet are not considered in the estimate. For illustration these men had yet to load a pair and a half of blankets, two pairs snowshoes, a bag of extra moccasins, socks, duffle, warm underclothes, extra trousers, coats, mits and a hundred and one other things which men penetrating the wilderness for several months may require.

In an expedition like this one must not think only of things necessary, but also things that may be required when a man is two or three hundred miles away from civilization and cuts his leg. He has no drug store to get plaster from. A full list of all a couple of prudent men have to take with them is quite interesting.

To resume, — these men left on the 10th of October and got back to the coast (on foot) the 12th of January, being absent almost exactly 3 months. They cached their traps, canoe and surplus things inland ready for the spring hunt.

After spending a fortnight with their families cutting wood and choring about their abodes they then went to work in the lumber camps for February and March. On April 15th they made a start for the interior once more, this time each hauling a flat sled loaded in equal weight with the following provisions: 80 lbs. pork, $10.00; 10 lbs. butter, $1.50; 180 lbs. flour, $3.20; 3 lbs. tea, $1.05; 12 lbs. sugar, 60 cts; 1 lb.

soda, 5 cts.; salt and pepper, 10 cts; $16.50.

With their other things this made a dead weight of about one hundred and eighty pounds per sled. On mixed ice and bush walking at the season when the snow is crusted a man will average, with such a load, twenty-five or thirty miles a day.

There are many hunters that are quite superstitious about parting with a single skin until the hunting or trapping season is over and then the whole collection is sold 'en-blac.' Other hunters again will sell their fall hunts less a skin. This reserved skin may be only a musquash. They keep this, as they say, to draw other skins when next they go trapping. The men I am writing about had no necessity to sell in the winter, and therefore kept all till the spring. The commencement of June is still considered spring in the North country.

The total catch and the prices realized are as follows: 38 martens at $10, $380; 10 mink at $2.50, $25; 1 beaver, $7; 2 bears at $7, $14; 3 bears at $20, $60; 4 fishers at $7, $28; 1 otter, $15; 120 musquash at 15c, $18; amount $547.00.

SUMMARY OF TRAPPING.

By total hunt, $547.00; to provisions, $49.50; sundries, 70 cts; 2 men's net earnings for 135 days at $1.84 equals $496.80.

The amount per diem clear to each of the brothers may not appear to the reader as very remunerative, yet compared to working in the shanties they did much better. The wages for good axe men last winter were from eighteen to twenty dollars per month.

Compared with the same length of time working in the lumber camps the figures would stand thus: 4½ months lumbering at average wages of $22 equals $99; 4½ months trapping, $248.40. In favor of trapping, say in round figures $150.00.

I submit the foregoing to the readers of H-T-T, hoping it may prove interesting.

*   *   *   *   *

It is no doubt ancient history, still it may be interesting to the readers to know the large hunts made by some of our Indians in the latter '60's. Referring to a note book kept in those days I find the hunt of one particular Indian recorded. His name was A-ta-so-kan — the only help he had, a boy of twelve.

This family left the Post in August and only returned the following June. His hunting grounds were just across the heights of lands going towards Hudson's Bay, from the headwaters of the Ottawa River. Game of all description was very plentiful then; so much so that, providing an Indian had a few pounds of flour and lard to get away from the vicinity of the station, his guns nets and snares kept him in abundance. A-ta-so-kan, altho having several children besides the boy took only fifty pounds of flour, ten pounds of lard, one pound of tea, and ten pounds of tobacco. Goods, however, he supplied himself well with — such as many of various bright-colored flannels, yards of duffle, yards of H. B. strouds, both blue and white, and several pairs of H. B. wool blankets. These people were brought up on country produce: i. e., fish and flesh, therefore found it no hardship to be without flour, etc., — the white man's food. From that one man and his young boy I got at the end of the hunting season (first of June) the following furs:

96	Large Beaver Skins.
226	Small Beaver Skins.
32	Otters.
120	Martens.
35	Minks.
40	Lynxes.
1236	Musquash.

Making altogether four of our eighty pound packs of furs. This, of course, was an exceptional hunt — still we had several other Indians who ran A-ta-so-kan a close second.

What a difference in the stretching and drying of that man's skins, compared with those we get on the frontier. Each skin, apart from the musquash, was as clean as note paper, all killed in season and all dried in the frost or shade. On the line of civilization there is such keen competition among the traders to get furs, that the hunters stretch and dry the skins in any way. Beaver, for instance, which is bought by the pound, is frequently weighted with syrup, and sand rubbed into the hair and paws, and considerable flesh left on, all tells when three or four dollars a pound is paid.

The Abanakis Indians about St. Francis Lake, St. Peter, are noted for their tricks of the trade, and when you get a blue-eyed Abanakis, look out to be cheated. I call to mind on the St. Maurice River, when stationed there, one of these gents brought furs to sell at our Post. Among the lot was a beaver skin. According to its size, if well dressed, it ought to have weighed a pound and a half, or three quarters at most. Judge of my surprise when I found it tipped the scales at two and half pounds. This was phenomenal and uncanny, and I remarked to the hunter, that we would leave the skins in the store until after dinner before closing the trade.

During the mid-day hour I slipped out and examined the skin critically, and found the rascal had flinched up layers of the inner skin or "cutem," and had inserted small sheets of tea-chest lead, after which he had pressed the skin down flat and dried it in this state. This was insult added to injury, because about a month previous he had begged the lead from me to make bullets with. Verily there are more tricks with horses and furs than meets the eye.

CHAPTER XXXII.

A PARD NECESSARY.

I say for safety, successful hunting, and division of the many necessary labors, when the hunting or trapping day is over, a proper partner is necessary. I am aware many old hunters have passed years quite alone in the solitude of the trackless forests and the valleys of the mountain ranges, but what a life! What risks they have run! Some may have led this life from choice or from greed to possess the whole proceeds of the trapping season; still it is a life no man should lead.

Sickness rarely overtakes a trapper; the outdoor life they practice is conducing to good health; continual exercise and fresh air engender a good appetite, but there is always the risk of accident, accident in many ways. The guns, the axe, the canoe, breaking through the ice, or even getting caught in one of his own traps; in fact by the last mentioned source of danger I have known two men to lose their lives in a most horrible way of torture and agony, and these men were not novices at the business; one was a middle-aged half-breed, born and brought up to trapping, and the other was an old Nova Scotian who had trapped and hunted for forty years and yet he died in a bear trap.

Man was not intended to live alone, and a trapper who passes the best part of his life far away from his fellow man becomes selfish, crabbed and morose. No matter how successful he may have been in his hunting years, when old age comes on, his last moments are generally passed alone in some miserable shanty, covered with dirty and musty old clothes and blankets, no one to pass him a drink of water or wipe the death sweat from his brow, or else some good person on the fringe of civilization, partly from charity or necessity, takes in the broken old hulk and keeps him until the end. A grave somewhere outside the fence is pointed out as where "Old Pierre," the trapper, is buried. I have several such resting places in my mind as I pen these lines.

No, I maintain a companion in hunting and trapping is a necessity in many ways. In selecting one they should be alike in only two points — age and honesty. If the head of the partnership is short, stout and of a phlegmatic nature, his chum ought to be say five feet ten inches high, weigh one hundred and fifty pounds, of a nervous energetic nature and cheerful. Two such men are most likely to get along well together.

Animals don't come to the camp door and ask to be skinned. On the contrary trapping, to do it right, is hard work and when the real day's work of tramping through swamps and over mountains setting traps is done there is yet much work for the cold, wet and hungry men to do at the camp; cutting and carrying the night's fire wood, cooking their supper, drying their clothes for the morrow, patching broken moccasins and skinning and stretching pelts they may have secured that day. With a good pard these labors are, of course, divided, and each cheerfully and silently takes his share.

There is nothing I have enumerated but what has to be done every night. A trapper returns to his camp, and if he has to make a new camp at the end of his trail so much more and harder is the work, and the poor old trapper without a companion must, of necessity, perform all these duties alone, the completion of which takes him far into the night. Brother trappers, I know whereof I write. I have tried both and I say for division of labor, for good comradeship and for positive safety select and join fortune with "A Good Pard."

To illustrate, I give one of my own experiences: I reached my camp once at dark in February, utterly tired out, wet by the melting snow on my clothes, and a fast that had not been broken at noon. There were a few burnt sticks in the fireplace (a lean to camp), these I raked together and started a blaze. With my excessive fatigue and the warmth of the fire, I fell asleep as I leaned for what I thought was a moment, against a stump in the camp. It was a dispensation of Providence that I ever awoke, but I did, far into that February night. On waking I realized in a moment the narrow escape that I had had. The great trees of the forest were cracking all about me with the intensity of the cold. My wet clothes were sticking to me as if of ice, but my brain was clear and I knew no time was to be lost in my self-preservation.

After tramping about and beating my body for some time to create circulation, I was rewarded by feeling my blood flow once more in a natural way. The last quarter of the moon shed what light it could over the tree tops and I strapped on my snowshoes and went to work at chopping wood to last till morning. A good cup of tea, some biscuit and pork and the then bright and cheerful fire made me my old self, but I received a lesson never to be forgotten.

CHAPTER XXXIII.
AN HEROIC ADVENTURE.

When we had come to anchor in Trinity Bay and all the sails were safely stowed, the captain of our yacht proposed we should go ashore and see the celebrated Comeau *fils*.

Bob, my companion asked, "Celebrated for what?"

"Oh! for several things," replied the captain. "He is a most extraordinary man in his many acquirements and knowledge. Born and brought up on this coast, he has passed all his life here, with the exception of the three years his father was able to send him to school, but those three years he made use of to lay the foundation of a wonderful store of practical knowledge. His schooling, as I have said, was but the foundation; by reading and observation he has added to it in a marvelous way.

"From his early training and the life of every one on the coast, it would go without saying that he knows how to shoot, but he is more than a good shot, he is a 'deadly' shot. Anything he aims his gun at that is within shooting distance is dead. As a salmon fisher, no crack angler who visits these rivers can hope to compete with him.

"As a linguist he can speak, read and write in French, English, Latin and Indian; besides this, he can talk rapidly in the dumb alphabet. He holds the position of telegraph operator at Trinity, also of postmaster and fishery overseer, and besides, when anything goes wrong with the line for two hundred miles east or west, the department immediately wires him to go and fix them up.

"He has more than a fair knowledge of medicine for one who derived all his insight from reading alone. Last summer there was an epidemic of measles all along the coast, among both whites and Indians. Here, with a population of 150, two-thirds of whom were down Comeau, who attended them, did not lose one patient, while at Bersimis, where the department sent a full-fledged M. D., there were thirty-nine burials out of a population of 450.

"You may be sure the poor people all along the coast love him."

So the boat was lowered away, and the Captain, Bob and I were rowed ashore to see this paragon. From the outside look of the place I could see the man was one of good taste and orderly. The knock at the door was answered by Comeau himself. The Captain was personally acquainted with him and introduced us before we entered. I must say I was disappointed. One always is when he has pictured a person in his mind's eye and finds that in reality he is quite a different kind of person.

I had looked for Comeau to be a large man and a boisterous one from his position of superiority over others. On the contrary, I found him below the medium, a quiet, low-voiced man, reserved almost to shyness. I saw at once he was a great observer, one who would make deductions from specks invisible to ordinary people; or, in other words, he could put two and two together and dovetail them better than most men.

We were ushered into a large, clean, airy room, in the middle of which sat a very good looking lady in a roomy rocker, with a child on each knee. If Comeau himself is reserved and not inclined to talk, his wife can do enough for both. She excused herself for not rising when her husband introduced us. Nodding down at her babies, she said, "You see I am fixed." One could see she is a proud mother — they are twins; this she told us before we were well seated, and she further informed us that they were the only twins on the Labrador. So she is celebrated also.

When we got fairly settled in Comeau's den, the conversation naturally drifted into hunting and fishing. Bob made some inquiries about the pools on the Trinity. To make his explanations clear, Comeau pulled out a drawer of photographic views of the river. In rummaging these over, he cast aside a gold medal. "Excuse me," I said, reaching over and taking up the medal. On it I read engraved:

"PRESENTED TO N. A. COMEAU BY THE R. H. S.
FOR BRAVERY IN SAVING LIFE."

Upon my asking him to recount the circumstances, he blushed and looked quite confused, and said: "Oh! it was nothing worth speaking of, but I suppose people talked so much about it that they gave me that token. It was nothing more than any man would have done," and this was all we could get from him unless we had carried persistency to an ungentlemanly degree.

After having spent a very pleasant hour, we returned on board, and the Captain told us the story that the hero himself would not:

Two years before, one day in January Comeau arrived home from the back country to find that two men had that day while seal hunting off shore been driven off the coast toward the ice pack in the gulf. One of the men was Comeau's own brother-in-law, and the other a half-breed. In spite of the supplications of his wife and the persuasions of the other individuals of the place, Comeau set about preparations to follow them out to sea. He asked no one to accompany him.

The wind all the afternoon had been steadily off shore and was now moderately calm. He took with him some restoratives, provisions, a lantern, a couple of blankets, his rifle and ammunition and what else useful he could think of in his hurry. The ice pack was then about ten miles off the land, and he reasoned the men must be on the ice, if large and strong enough, or in among it if in small cakes, the latter being much more dangerous.

From Trinity to Matane in a direct line the distance is forty-five miles, and to push out in a frail, wooden canoe alone and the darkness coming on in the black gulf in mid-winter required a brave man with extraordinary nerve to dare it, and this Comeau did.

Three minutes after pushing out from the beach, canoe and man were swallowed up in the darkness. The next the people of Trinity heard of him was a telegraphic message on the second day after. It read: "Matane. All three alive. Joseph, hands frozen; Simon, both feet frozen badly."

This message was to his family, but the Matane people sent a much longer one to the government, giving the facts, describing the hardships these men had come through, and a special train was sent down with the best surgeon from Quebec. On the surgeon's arrival at Matane a consultation was held with the county practitioner, when it was decided that the man Joseph would have to lose two fingers on each hand and Simon both feet.

The amputation was successfully carried out next day, and shortly after, when Comeau saw both men well on to recovery, he started for his home, not, however, by the way he had come, but up to Quebec by the south shore and down the north shore from Quebec, a distance of nearly 700 miles. The last hundred he made on snowshoes.

The Captain told us that the description of this very venturesome trip he had heard from Comeau's own brother as the elder one had described it in the heart of his own family. He had reached the ice pack, to the best of his judgment, about fifteen miles from the land, and had remained on his oars and hallowed once or twice without receiving an answer. He suddenly bethought himself of the lantern. This he lit and lashed to the blade of one of his oars, and erected it aloft. Immediately a faint cry was heard to the eastward, and he lowered his light and pulled away in the direction whence the call appeared to come. After rowing for a short time the lantern was waved above again, and this time an answering shout came from close at hand.

The two poor fellows were some distance in the pack, and had got on the largest cake they could find. They were sitting there helpless, holding on each by one hand to the rough surface of the ice, and with the other to their canoe to keep it from being washed off.

By the aid of the lantern held aloft, Comeau saw there was a much larger cake of ice some distance further in the pack. To this they made their way with laborious trouble. Pushing one canoe as far ahead among the ice as possible, they would all three get into this, shove the other in advance in the same way, and so repeating the process till they reached the solid field. Once safely on this, for the meantime, secure place, food was partaken of and daylight waited for.

Soon, however, the intense cold began to make itself felt, and drowsiness was fast taking hold of the two men, and their great wish was to be left alone and allowed to sleep. This Comeau knew if indulged meant death, and it took all his efforts to keep them awake and moving about. Once while attending to the halfbreed, his brother-in-law dropped down and was fast asleep in an instant. Comeau boxed him, kicked him, without having the desired effect of rousing him from his stupor. At last he bethought him of what an old Indian had done to him under somewhat similar circumstances. He caught the man's nose between the thumb and finger and tweaked it severely. This brought him to his feet and mad to fight.

Day was now breaking, and they could see the south shore at a computed distance of ten miles. Comeau also saw that the ice pack was drifting steadily east, and this, if they remained on the ice, would carry them past Cap Chat, the most northern point of the south coast, and this meant death to a certainty.

A rapid train of thought went through Comeau's brain. He decided that if saved they were to be, it must be by passing over that ten miles of moving, grinding ice. He forced some food on the others and gave each a small dram of spirits; how much rather would he have given them tea or coffee. But even if he had had it, water was wanting to make it. They abandoned the roll of blankets, which had been of no use to them, and started, using the canoes see-saw fashion as they had done the night before. They left the cake of ice upon which they had passed the night at 8 A. M. and only got ashore at the extreme point of Cap Chat at daylight next morning. At times they would come across narrow lanes of water, but these lanes always ran at right angles to the direction in which they were going. Several times, when stepping upon what was considered a strong piece of ice, one of the party would be immersed in the cold, cruel water, and be rescued with great trouble and danger to the others.

What a picture of heartfelt prayer offering it must have been, to have seen those men kneeling on the ice-bound shore, pouring out their thanks to the ever-watchful Almighty who had brought them safely through such dangers.

*   *   *   *   *

Bob, who had taken down the Captain's narrative in shorthand, gave me his notes, and I give the story of adventure and heroism to the public.

Comeau is well known by most of the members of the Forest and Stream clubs of New York and Montreal.

CHAPTER XXXIV.

WILD OXEN.

I read in one of the May issues of *Forest and Stream* of a dog that joined a band of wolves and became as savage and fleet of foot as the best of them, and brought to my mind a circumstance that came under my own observation, of a pair of steers that threw off all trammels of restraint and took to the bush.

I think it is worth recording, for it shows that even horned cattle brought up with care, and fed at regular intervals can support themselves, even through the rigor of a northern winter in the wild bush country.

In my early days on the Labrador we were in the habit of getting our winter beef on the hoof from the villages on the south shore. The cattle were sent over by schooner, late in the fall, and stall-fed until the cold weather set in, when they were killed and the carcasses hung up to freeze. As we had no wharf accommodation, the cattle were unloaded in a primitive and unceremonious way. The schooner anchored two or three hundred yards from the shore. The cattle sided up alongside the rail next the beach, and a couple of sailors introduced hand spikes under the animal's body, the end engaging the top of the rail. At the word "Go" the beasts were hurled sideways into the water. Rising to the surface, after the plunge, they naturally struck out for the shore, where we had men with short ropes ready to secure them and lead them away to the stable.

On the occasion upon which I write we had a consignment of five three-year-old steers, the meat of which, augmented by the usual game of the country, was considered sufficient for the post's use during the following winter.

Two of the bunch reached footing in such a lively state that they baffled the combined efforts of our men to capture them, and with a few defiant snorts and bounds, they reached the primitive forest and were lost to view.

As soon as I realized that there was a possibility of the animals being lost to us, I turned out all the "hangers on" about the post, with our own men in hot pursuit. Night coming on shortly after, the hunt was given up, only to be resumed with greater energy the following day; but the nature of the ground being hard, hoof marks were indistinguishable, and to use dogs would only make the cattle wilder. Once more the men had to reluctantly abandon the search and return to the post, and although we kept up the hunt for several days more, we failed to locate the missing "meat."

In due course of time, snow covered the ground, and men circled the bush in the vicinity of the post without any results, and we had unwillingly to place the two steers on our profit and loss account.

Time went on, the winter passed, and the summer also, and none of the visiting Indians reported any signs of the cattle.

The following winter, in February, a party of hunters came in from the headwaters of the Moisie River, 150 miles north of us, and they reported having killed our cattle among a small herd of wood caribou. To prove their story they produced the horns which they had brought down all those miles on their toboggans as visible proof.

The report they gave me was as follows: They had come across the tracks of this small bunch of caribou (five) with which the oxen were living in consort, sometime in early December. The animals winded them and the hunters failed to sight the herd.

As the snow was yet shallow, they left them unmolested until after the New Year, when the men from the nearby camps organized a hunt expressly to run them down.

From hearsay they thought the strange tracks were those of moose, and were very much, surprised when the herd was sighted to find they were horned cattle, and at once concluded (and very correctly) that they were the long lost cattle.

The chief informed me they were so fleet of foot that the five deer were come up with and killed before they overtook the steers, which were rolling fat, sleek of coat and had an under growth of wool such as the deer had, showing that under different circumstances nature had given them this protection against the severity of the climate.

I hardly think I would have credited their story with the proof, and further, the next summer, when they came in to trade on the coast, they brought me a piece of the thigh skin of each animal. Verily these oxen had a call from the wild and took it and became as one with the denizens of the bush.

Reading of the dog that fraternized and went off with the wolves brought this to my mind after a lapse of forty-one years.

CHAPTER XXXV.
LONG LAKE INDIANS.

The two years I passed in charge of the Hudson's Bay Post of Long Lake, situated on the water-shed between Lake Superior and Hudson's Bay, was the happiest of any period of my long service.

The conclusion I have arrived at, after considerable experience, is that Christianizing, in no matter what form, has only made the Indian worse.

It is the verdict of all who have had to do with the red man, that he copies all of the white man's vices and very few, if any, of his virtues.

Indians I found at Long Lake, in the middle seventies, were Pagans, but they were honest, truthful and virtuous.

We locked our tradeshop, not to prevent robbery, simply to guard against the door being blown open. Not one of these Indians would have taken a pin without showing it to me first and saying: "I am going to keep this," holding up the pin.

My predecessor had been stationed at that post in an unbroken charge of over twenty years. He was a man of system and everything went by rote. There were certain fixed dates for out-fitting the hunters; certain dates for those short of ammunition to come and get it in the winter; and, best of all, certain dates for them to arrive in the spring and close their hunts. This assured us of getting only prime, seasoned skins, and such skins it was a pleasure to handle, since the paper upon which this is printed is not whiter than every skin that passed thru my hands in those two years.

I am writing of the days before the Canadian Pacific Railway passed thru that country when there were no whiskey peddlers going about demoralizing the Indians. There being no opposition we regulated the catch of furs. When we found, by general report of the hunters, that a certain kind of fur was becoming scarce, we lowered the price for that particular animal's pelt so low as to not make it worth their while to trap it. For instance, while I was there, the beaver was having our protection, and, as a consequence, in three years every little pond or creek became stocked with beaver. The Indian hunter did not suffer, because we paid the most liberal prices for the skins that were most plentiful. This policy, however, could only be carried out at places where there was no competition.

The gentleman in charge was the representative of the "Great Company" and what he said was law. Our interests and those of the Indians ran on parallel lines.

It was to our interest to see all that the Indian required should be of the very best. That he should have good, strong, warm clothing, good ammunition and double-tower proved guns was essential to his ability to hunt, his comfort and his very life.

It was drilled into the hunters at each yearly send off, that if he did not exert himself to hunt sufficient to pay the advances given him, that the "Great Father" would not, or could not, send goods for the next year.

It was explained to them that their furs were bartered in far off countries for other new guns, blankets, twine, capots, duffle, copper kettles and other wants of the Indians. As we wanted the hunters to be well clothed and supplied with necessaries we imported no such useless trash as the frontier posts were obliged to keep to cope with the free traders.

If an Indian took a four point H. B. blanket, even with the rough usage it was subjected to, it would keep him and his wife warm for a year. The next season, a new one being bought, the old one did service for another winter as lining for mittens, strips for socks, and leggings for the younger branches.

Steel traps being dear twenty-five years ago, and the long canoe transport being costly so far into the interior, we did not import them very largely.

Bears, martens, minks and even beaver and otter were killed in deadfalls; and with different sizes of twine, the Indians snared rabbits, lynx, and, in the spring, even the bear.

The Indians principal, and I may say, only tools for hunting and for his support were his axe, ice chisel, twine and his gun. I mention the gun last because the hunter only used it for caribou and moose, ducks and geese. Ammunition was too costly to use it for anything that could be trapped or snared.

A life chief was elected by the Indians themselves, and he was supported in his management of the tribe by the officer in charge of the post. The chief had precedence in being outfitted, his canoe headed the fleet of canoes on arriving at the post in the spring, and was the one to lead off in the autumn. His was the only pack of furs carried up from the beach, by our men, to the store, and he set the example to his young men by being the first to pay his last year's advances. To him we gave, as a present, a new suit of black cloth clothes, boots, hat, etc., and to his wife a bright tartan wool dress piece, and a tartan shawl of contrasting pattern.

Our currency, or medium of trade, was called "Made Beaver," equivalent in most articles to a dollar. The value of each skin was computed in "Made Beaver." For every hundred of "Made Beaver" of skins that the Indian brought in we allowed him as a gratuity "Called Rum," ten "Made Beaver," he was at liberty, after paying his debt, to trade whatever he fancied out of the shop to the extent of his "Rum." But unless he paid his debt in full the "Rum" he was entitled to went towards his account. This, however, seldom happened, because one that did not pay his debt in full was looked down upon by his friends, and his supplies for the next year were reduced in proportion to his deficiency.

What a change has taken place in the past quarter of a century. I hear from the person now in charge of that post (it is kept up principally now to protect our further interior post) that all those Indians are dead and gone. Their descendants number scarcely one-third of the original band. They are thieves, drunkards and liars as a rule; the white man's diseases and fire-water have left their trail. White trappers have penetrated their country in all directions from the line of railway and exterminated most of the fur-bearing animals. Instead of, as their forefathers, getting a good supply of all necessary articles to assure them of comfort for a year, these, their sons and grandsons, can get no one to risk advancing them. They live principally, now, on fish and when they do succeed in killing a skin, the most likely thing to happen is, they will travel many miles to barter it for whiskey.

This is one of the results of railways and civilization. I can say with the late lamented Custer "The good Indians are dead."

CHAPTER XXXVI.

DEN BEARS.

A phase of hunting that I do not remember ever seeing described in the H-T-T is of tracking bears to their den and killing them there. The two seasons that this mode of hunting is resorted to by the Indians is after the first fall of snow and again in February, March or April, according to the different locality of the country, when the snow is soft and the days are mild and spring-like. Some very knowing trailers will follow up signs even before there is snow on the ground. They watch out for broken branches, shredded birch bark or other stuff which the bear has torn down to make his bed.

At times, however, the bear will change his mind, even after considerable work has been done, and move off to some other ridge of hills and there begin over again in what he has decided a more favorable situation. It is a much more dangerous job to tackle a newly denned bear than in the spring when they are stupid from their long spell of hibernation. Rarely does a lone hunter undertake to kill a bear in his den. It requires two persons for safety and convenience of work.

In hunting out a bear's den a knowledge of what is a likely locality shortens the work very much. There are dens found in freak and unlooked for places, but as a general rule there are certain conditions that go towards their selection and one who knows these, narrows down his area of hunting very considerably.

The dens are, as a rule, on a high elevation with a southern aspect. This selection is made, no doubt, with the knowledge given by instinct that it keeps clear longer in the autumn and opens earlier with the melting snows of spring. In my long experience I have found bears three times in very unlikely places. One time, when on a long trail with dispatches, two Indians and myself jumped, one after the other, from the trunk of a large fallen pine, with our snow shoes, fair and square onto a very large bear who had in the fall made his bed at the lea side of this shelter and allowed the winter snows to fall and bury him.

It was only three weeks later when we were returning by the same trail that the leading man of the party, when getting to this spot and looking for an easy place to clamber up onto the giant trunk noticed a suspiciously frosted little breathing hole in the snow. Word was passed back that perhaps there was a bear there. As we had no firearms in the party not even a pistol, the first thing to do was to cut good stout hardwood poles about five feet long.

A large place was well tramped down with our snow shoes to insure good solid footing and when all was ready, with our packs and extra things out of the way, one of the party was detailed to get up on the tree trunk and with a strong birch lever insert it near where we located the bear to be and pry him out, the other two to belabor him with their poles. The man on the log had such a strong leverage that his first effort broke the bear clear out of the snow and before he had time to rouse from his stupor he was dead.

The Indians, who were middle-aged men, thought it a great joke that we should all have tramped on this bear and three weeks later found and killed him. The skin, of course, was at its primest state, so we packed it turn and turn about, to the fort, where each received his share of its value.

Another time I camped almost on the very shore of a small lake with a youth for my companion. We were to start a yard of moose in the early morning on a mountain on the opposite shore. In the morning while I was cooking breakfast, the youth went a few yards away to cut a pole to hang our extra provisions on that we were leaving at the camp.

He had hardly left the fireplace when I heard him call me. There I found him gazing intently at a telltale frosted hole in the snow. We both came to the same conclusion that it was the breathing hole of some animal and that animal most likely a bear. We decided not to disturb him until our moose hunt was over, so quietly withdrew from the vicinity. I may say to close this incident that two days later, after killing three moose, we dug out the bear sufficiently to locate his shoulder and shot him in his den.

Another unlocked for place was when landing at a portage very late in the fall, was to find a half-sized bear had made his bed simply at the foot of a stump. There was no snow yet on the ground and he woke sufficiently to gaze on us with a stupid stare. The next minute he had his quietus.

I always seem to wander away from my subject. Whether it adds or detracts from the interest of the article I know not, but I assure the reader it is unintentional, but these long past incidents and adventures will crop up in my memory and before I think to pull myself up they are committed to paper. Well, once again!

The most likely places to find a bear denned up are under a ledge of rocks, under the roots of a partly fallen tree, under an over-hanging sand bank, or in a rocky crevice in the mountain side. The hunters, when they have tracked him to or found his den begin by reading all the visible signs and lay their plans accordingly. If the bed is some little distance back from the door or opening, they begin by staking up the doorway so nearly closed that the bear will have considerable delay in getting out.

If to stake it is impracticable on account of the formation, they gather rocks or sections of logs and stuff up most of the opening. Some venturesome hunters will stand a leg at each side of the opening with their axe poised ready to brain him while he is endeavoring to make his exit, the man's companion prodding him out from the rear. Other hunters (the writer amongst them) prefer to remain with his rifle ready for business at a few yards from the doorway. This is safer and more reasonable.

Most bears come out into daylight in a more or less dazed state, but I have known some with the very first introduction of the pole into the rear premises to come out with a rush, carrying obstructions and everything before them. At such times unless a man is pretty nervy he is apt to get "Bear Fever" and he should not be blamed, for the situation is trying.

When the bear has taken up his quarters far back in a crevice of the rocks where a pole from the surface can find no opening to be introduced, then the plan of smoking him out has to be resorted to. It is done in this way. The stuff to be used, some birch bark to ignite it on top of which is placed rotten wood or broken up punk if procurable, is rammed back a distance into the hole. At the end of the withdrawn pole a lighted twist of bark is pushed back and the doorway quickly blocked as nearly tight as possible.

The hunter retires at once to a safe distance with his gun ready for action and awaits events. He does not, as a rule, have to wait long, for when that smoke becomes unbearable, Mr. Bear comes out in a hurry and a pretty mad bear at that. It is not advisable to introduce too much inflammable substance, for it is apt to spoil the fur when the bear comes thru the fiery ordeal. Rotten popple is next to punk to make a pungent and unbearable smoke. When such penetrates the bear's nostrils he is bound to wake up and his one desire is to get fresh air immediately.

The tracking of a bear even in pretty deep snow takes time, for unless he knows some one is after him he circles and zigzags about, which trail requires attention to under run successfully. However, once he becomes possessed with the knowledge that he is being pursued, he makes a pretty straight line away from danger. At such a time a small cur dog is invaluable, for while he will not attack the bear, by his yelping and barking he delays his progress and at each pause of the bear the hunter is gaining ground.

To kill a bear that is already denned the dog is better left at home, for he will be of no use and you run the risk (if he is plucky) of his being killed in the den. For all kinds of hunting I have found the small dog much preferable to the one of large size. A small dog can readily be put in one's game bag and carried up near the game one is to start. He is lighter and takes up less room in a canoe, the bones and scraps of the camp are sufficient for his support, he will run in and nip at the heels of a moose or deer and get out of the way and repeat his barking, while a big dog would be getting into trouble and endangering his life.

I have often carried my hunting dog in my game bag up a mountain and only slipped him when the moose had jumped his bed. The dog being fresh he very soon had the moose at a standstill. In hunting bear the small dog has the discretion to keep out of his reach and be contented with barking and running him around. Whereas the bigger dogs are fearless and run in on the quarry generally with fatal results to themselves, for there is no modern pugilist quicker with his fists than a bear with his paw, and let the bear get but one good whack at a dog and that dog is no better thereafter than a dead dog.

CHAPTER XXXVII.

THE MISHAPS OF RALSON.

Among the many young apprentice officers who have been under my orders in the Hudson's Bay Company, none was so conspicuously unfortunate as Ralson. His bungling into trouble became so frequent that it got to be a byword amongst the other clerks and employes and at last they came to me and said, "Mr. Hunter, you ought really to forbid Ralson's going outside the stockades unless some one is along to take care of him."

For the short while he was in our service (three years) he had, as far as I know, the record for varied mishaps. These were of so frequent occurrence that at the end of his contract he was allowed to leave and, by my advice, he returned to his people in England. Good luck appeared to go hand in hand with his misadventures, for somehow he came out alive, still, to say the least, the uncertainty every time he left the post as to whether he would return, kept one's nerves forever on the ragged edge and notwithstanding, he quickly became an adept at most work connected with the service. I was glad to see him leave the service because, being under my orders and not yet to man's estate, I considered myself in a great measure responsible for his safety.

I call to memory his having almost cut off the index finger of his left hand, putting the axe right thru the knuckle joint. This bled profusely and he was on the sick list for a long while. I think the next accident very shortly after his hand healed, was to put the corner of his axe into the cap of his knee. This was more serious than the other and took weeks to get well. On the whole he was very fortunate not to have a stiff leg for the remainder of his life.

Another time he undertook to look for a man who was over-due at the post and was expected to come by a trail near the lake shore. This was a case of the biter being bitten, for the man turned up all right and had to join a party to hunt Ralson. As he told us afterwards he thought to improve on the trail by cutting curves. Dusk coming on he became hopelessly lost himself, neither being able to find the trail nor his way out of the forest. The search party only found him the following afternoon, tattered, hungry and generally woe-begone. A picture of him taken as he entered the square that day would have been interesting.

The chances are that he might never have been found and thus have perished, had a quieting effect on him for some days but the old restlessness got hold of him again, and he had to be away hunting up fresh trouble. This time he had a companion and they went in a canoe to hunt ducks. His companion (a half-breed) debarked on the river bank to crawl up to some birds and placed an injunction on Ralson to remain quietly seated in the canoe. When the half-breed returned to the river bank it was to find the canoe upset and Ralson sitting on the shore dripping wet. On comparing notes it was found a rifle I had lent him was at that precise moment at the bottom of the river in about ten feet of water.

It would never do to return to the post and report this mishap and the loss of the gun, so Ralson undressed and began to dive for its recovery. Robert, the man, told me, when describing the adventure, that he never laughed so much in his life as when sitting on the bank and watching Ralson making desperate and repeated efforts to recover the weapon. He was finally successful and exacted a cast iron promise from Robert not to inform the people at the post. A promise which Robert promptly broke.

An accident, however, which almost cost him his life, altho after he was safe at the post, caused us considerable merriment, came about in this way, and I expect he will remember it as long as he lives, if yet alive. We were sending an express canoe from the post to the nearest point on the frontier to mail dispatches to headquarters. The distance is about fifty miles over lakes, rivers and portages. The usual time for such a trip was three days for the round trip. Ralson begged to accompany the men, partly for an outing and partly to see the frontier village of Luqueville.

Their route lay thru a chain of small lakes on which I had a couple of bear traps set. To save me a trip to visit these traps I told Robert, the guide, to kill any bear he found caught and reset the traps, cache the meat and skin and bring it with them on their return journey. These instructions were simple enough and I was not anxious about Ralson. Ralson, however, changed all these plans for, when they reached the first trap, in which they found a bear caught and Robert had killed it, Ralson proposed he should stay behind, skin and cut up the meat and visit the second trap which was a short distance off the canoe route, and then he was to come home on foot by skirting the lakes along a sometimes used trail, taking the skin with him.

Robert thought this plan a good one as it would expedite matters for he and his companion to make a quick trip. When, however, he got back to the place after an absence of about forty hours and found the skin and meat lying where he had left them and no sign of Ralson, he was quick to understand that something had happened. What that something was, however, he was at a loss to settle in his mind. All at once, while standing there considering, the thought struck him that possibly Ralson was caught in the other trap. Such things had happened to men accustomed to trapping and how much more likely to a careless fellow like the missing man.

Giving expression to his thought Robert and his companion both hurried off towards the other trap, which was about a mile up the creek. When they came to a soft place on the trail and saw only the footprints of a man going and none returning, Robert was convinced the poor fellow was in the trap, whether alive or dead they refrained from contemplating. What a sight met their gaze when coming in sight of the bear pen! There was poor Ralson lying prone on his back motionless and to all appearances dead, the great, heavy mass of metal fast to his leg and his pocket knife with broken blade lying near at hand, evidently thrown there as useless. They saw how he had hacked at the strong birch drag to which the chain was fastened until his knife became useless and then given up in despair.

Ralson, upon examination, was found to be yet alive, but unconscious and covered with blue flies, his hands and face were swollen from the mosquito poison and covered with dirt he had scratched while trying to dig for water. He looked a frightful and pitiful object. Luckily the men who had found him were quick to think and in a remarkably short space of time they had the leg freed from its iron clasp. One ran for a pannikin of cold water while the other twisted a piece of birch bark into the shape of a horn, with the small end open just enough to allow the water to trickle thru gently into his throat.

Next they bathed and washed his face and hands and shortly had the satisfaction of seeing him open his eyes. Robert now held up his head and placed the remaining water in the pannikin to his lips. This he managed to drink and blessed, blessed water, it revived him completely. The other man was then sent back to the canoe for the tea kettle and provisions, Robert starting a fire during his absence. Tea and partridge broth made and administered in small quantities at first helped him to regain his strength. His youthful vitality soon asserted itself and after he was propped up and made comfortable he managed to feed himself with some of the shredded meat.

After partaking of this food and drink the boot was cut off, the poor swollen foot bathed and bound up and then they carried him on an improvised stretcher very carefully and tenderly out to the canoe. Excepting two short portages it was all water way to the post at which place they arrived just at dusk. Souder, our cook, when he saw them helping Ralson out of the canoe said, "Mein Gott! Vich end of Ralson is sick dis time? Can't you tole me, eh?" and it was pretty hard to tell from his limp appearance.

After he had recovered sufficiently to be questioned as to how he got into the trap he said he had reached into the back of the house to affix the bait and forgot the trap and stepped into it. The meat that he had cut up was, of course, spoiled, but the skin after being washed and scraped, proved to have sustained no damage.

Ralson had no further mishaps in this country for when his foot was healed he took his discharge and returned to a well-off mother in London who could afford to have a keeper to care for him if so inclined. This happened years ago and as I never heard from him he may have joined the English Yeomanry and gone to South Africa and been killed on the firing line. If so, his mishaps are finished and so is my story.

END OF CANADIAN WILDS.

Lector House believes that a society develops through a two-fold approach of continuous learning and adaptation, which is derived from the study of classic literary works spread across the historic timeline of literature records. Therefore, we aim at reviving, repairing and redeveloping all those inaccessible or damaged but historically as well as culturally important literature across subjects so that the future generations may have an opportunity to study and learn from past works to embark upon a journey of creating a better future.

This book is a result of an effort made by Lector House towards making a contribution to the preservation and repair of original ancient works which might hold historical significance to the approach of continuous learning across subjects.

HAPPY READING & LEARNING!

LECTOR HOUSE LLP
E-MAIL: lectorpublishing@gmail.com